Routledge Revivals

MONGOLIAN JOURNEY

MONGOLIAN JOURNEY

HENNING HASLUND

First published in 1949 by Routledge and Kegan Paul Ltd

This edition first published in 2018 by Routledge
2 Park Square, Milton Park, Abingdon, Oxon, OX14 4RN
and by Routledge
52 Vanderbilt Avenue, New York, NY 10017, USA

Routledge is an imprint of the Taylor & Francis Group, an informa business

© 1949 by Taylor and Francis

All rights reserved. No part of this book may be reprinted or reproduced or utilised in any form or by any electronic, mechanical, or other means, now known or hereafter invented, including photocopying and recording, or in any information storage or retrieval system, without permission in writing from the publishers.

Publisher's Note
The publisher has gone to great lengths to ensure the quality of this reprint but points out that some imperfections in the original copies may be apparent.

Disclaimer
The publisher has made every effort to trace copyright holders and welcomes correspondence from those they have been unable to contact.
A Library of Congress record exists under ISBN: 68076141

ISBN 13: 978-0-367-15175-1 (hbk)
ISBN 13: 978-0-367-15177-5 (pbk)
ISBN 13: 978-0-429-05549-2 (ebk)

MONGOLIAN
JOURNEY

By the same Author

TENTS IN MONGOLIA
MEN AND GODS IN MONGOLIA
MORE TRAVELS IN MONGOLIA

HENNING HASLUND

MONGOLIAN

JOURNEY

LONDON
ROUTLEDGE & KEGAN PAUL LTD

ASIATISKE STREJFTOG *first published in Denmark, 1946*

MONGOLIAN JOURNEY *first published in England by*
ROUTLEDGE AND KEGAN PAUL LTD
Broadway House, 68-74 Carter Lane, London, E.C.4
1949

Translated from the Danish
by F. H. LYON

PRINTED IN GREAT BRITAIN BY HEADLEY BROTHERS
109 KINGSWAY, LONDON, W.C.2 AND ASHFORD, KENT

CONTENTS

	PAGE
PREFACE	ix
WHY DID WE SET OUT?	1
FROM SINGAPORE TO SHANGHAI	4
FROM SHANGHAI TO PEKING	13
THE GIRL WHO PAINTED A FAN	23
IN THE HEART OF JASAKTU LAND	36
THE PRINCESS'S TEMPLE	46
IN CAMP AT MANCHU AIL	59
AMONG DEVIL DANCERS IN THE KING'S MONASTERY	68
STEPPE POETRY	80
THE YOUNGER GENERATION OF MONGOLIA	91
CHRISTMAS NIGHT IN THE WILD	101
THE MONGOLS' "BLUE CITY"	111
WITH FIRE-WORSHIPPERS IN MONGOLIA	121
THE HOLY FIRE MAIDEN	132
THE WHITE OLD MAN OF THE STEPPE	139
TO A WEDDING FEAST AMONG THE CHAHAR PEOPLE	153
A NOMAD'S FUNERAL	165
ROBBER LIFE IN MONGOLIA	177

CONTENTS

ON CHRISTIAN SOIL IN A HEATHEN LAND . . . 189

THE OASIS BEYOND THE DESERT 197

IN THE LAND OF SNOW 208

EAST IS EAST . . . ? 220

INDEX 227

PLATES

AT END OF BOOK

	PLATE
MANCHU PRINCESS	I
MONGOL CHIEF	II
A BRIDE'S DOWRY	III-VI
WARRIOR, TROUBADOUR, SHEPHERD, SHEPHERDESS, STORY-TELLER, BOWMAN, LAMA, PILGRIM, HEADMAN OF CAMP, WIFE, SON, DAUGHTER-IN-LAW, UNMARRIED GIRL, THE YOUNGER GENERATION, CARAVAN LEADER, HUNTER, NOVICE, *HAIKH-LAMA, GURTUM*, THE GIRL FROM NIJA, THE WHITE OLD MAN OF THE STEPPE .	VII-XII
MAP SHOWING REGIONS AND PLACES MENTIONED IN *Mongolian Journey*	END OF BOOK

PREFACE

THE Mongol Lodai is the master who did the illustrations to this book. Throughout the summer of 1938 Lodai stayed at my quarters in the Mongols' "Blue City". The many drawings of galloping horsemen, archers, and other Mongolian figures and situations, which flowed in a lively stream from his China ink brush, revealed to me a great deal in the life of Central Asia which I might otherwise have overlooked.

He was an artist of the classical Central Asiatic school, a late offshoot of the form of art which Alexander the Great brought to Hindustan more than two thousand years ago.

Lodai's masterly drawings inspired me to order a bookplate from him. After much reflection he set about the work, the result of which is seen on the half-title of this book. The fabulous beast depicted is called in Mongolian "Arselan", and the Mongols use this word in their endeavours to pronounce my Danish name. Beside the lion-like fabulous beast, Lodai drew the letters and signs which correspond phonetically to my Danish name in Mongolian, Tibetan and Chinese. I had to type my name as a model for the Latin characters.

PREFACE

After Lodai had apparently finished his work, he sat for a long time absorbed in silent contemplation of it. But suddenly a broad, happy smile spread over his face, and he began to draw again. When he had finished, I asked if I might see the picture. I asked what the little Arselan which he had added in one corner signified. He smiled slyly and pointed to the happy family photograph which hung over my sleeping-bag. "And I have altered the muzzles of the two Arselans so that there can be no doubt whom they symbolize", he added, his eyes beaming with pride and fun.

So it happened that my son Sören came to appear on my bookplate in the form of a little lion cub, trotting along cheerfully with turned-up nose in his father's footsteps.

The drawings on pages 35, 68, 124, 145, and 177, as well as those on Plates III-VI, were done by Miss Inger Achton from originals brought home to the National Museum by the author. The pictures on pages 23, 29, 33 and 34 are from old Chinese woodcuts.

All the photographs were taken by the author in 1936-37 and 1938-39.

WHY DID WE SET OUT?

WHY did we set out—I and those of like mind with me—for the world which lies beyond the limits reached by civilization's boldest cables and railway lines?

There was so much that lured us—the desire to see what was hidden on the other side of the farthest of all known passes; the urge to test our qualities on tasks which were something else than just going on in a rut, as old people do; the longing to use young and untried muscles in a game which promised adventures and great experiences.

The first time we started out in search of the adventurous world of our desires, we only made the leap which ninety per cent. of all youth in all times has dreamed of in its healthiest hours. And if we reached the goal of our dreams, there where time is counted by sunrises and full moons, where the hurrying hands of a watch come to a stop, we inevitably struck root there. For

> " the man who has had the desert for his pillow, and lived in the day-dreamers' silent world, longs and longs to return . . . .".

WHY DID WE SET OUT?

We are a little band who meet now and again here at home to call up unforgettable memories—bronze-gold wild horses against the blue flats of Gaz Köl, the charming silhouettes of Orongo antelopes against Tibet's lofty skies, the unknown princess who smiled at us from her thousand-year-old death-bed in the desert sand. Or we meet out there at a camp fire in the wild to listen to the natives' old-world talk and to experience once more the quiet and grandeur of nature, which wake and nourish new thoughts and feelings. . . .

And why do we ever seek new passes, sunsets, camp fires? Not to gain honour and easily won riches, for out there not so much as a safe pension is to be had. But if one climbs the right peaks one sees with the right eyes, and if one listens to the right voices, one has a chance of finding one's own lucky stone.

I learnt this first from one of my old uncles, who as lately as seven years ago could tell how he had cleared the ground for his tent on the spot where Leopoldville now stands. Uncle Albert was Stanley's right-hand man on the expedition which resulted in the foundation of the Congo State; he was the first man to navigate a paddle steamer up the Congo's swift stream; and he was the first white man to look out over Leopold II's lake far into the dark continent of Africa.

When Uncle Albert was seventy-seven years old, I asked him one day if he had never regretted the many years of his youth he had spent among savages and wild beasts in the pestilential Congo jungles. He sat in thought for a few moments; then he took me into his Spartan bedroom in the little flat on the Aa Boulevard. The bed, like everything he had about him, was clean and neat, but the white sheets were covered with little patches and darns, and there were even a few small holes with round burnt edges.

"Look here, my boy," said Uncle Albert, running his hand gently over the holes and patches in the sheet, " every evening, when it gets dark, the noise of the town begins to disturb my thoughts. So I shut my window to keep out the noise of the trams, pull down the blinds to hide all those flickering coloured advertisements, go to bed with a good cigar, and in my thoughts I make a pilgrimage to *my* Africa. I hear the rushing of the Congo and all the mysterious noises of the primæval forest. I have pleasant talks with free heathens, who have not yet been forced into the parti-coloured cotton shirt of civilization.

" In the smoke of my good cigar I glimpse all the thoughts and mental pictures I hardly dare to call up in the cynical daylight of civilization—and I revive happy memories.

" Next morning a new hole has been burnt in my sheet ; but all these little holes, darns and patches are dear to me— they are a fine pattern of good memories. When my hands fumble over them in the dark, the medicine man who once saved my life beats his drum ; the black chief who was once a true friend to me clasps my hand in a firm grip ; and all the spirits of the wild croon delicious tunes to which I shall enjoy listening when some day I smoke my last cigar."

FROM SINGAPORE TO SHANGHAI

Singapore, Hongkong and Shanghai!

TO-DAY these beautiful names evoke in our imagination gloomy pictures of war, and the memories which once they awoke of many delightful adventures are overclouded by the thought of all the misery these places have had to undergo in the past months.[1]

There was a time when it was believed that civilization had brought good to these distant places. Singapore, " Lions' Island ", which at the beginning of the last century had been a fever-stricken marsh and a resort of cruel pirates, was now transformed into a great trading-place, where the splendours of East and West were exchanged ; here, where earlier only a scanty fishing population had existed precariously, hundreds of thousands of the surplus population of the East could live in good conditions.

[1] With reference to this, and a number of subsequent passages in the book, it should be noted that they were written before the defeat of Japan and her expulsion from the territories seized by her in the war, and also from those which she had previously occupied on the mainland of Asia.

Hongkong, " Valley of the Scented Waters "—in our grandfathers' time a barren, desolate rock—was now changed to a paradise where trade flourished on a large scale, and whither tens of thousands of the unfortunate population of China had fled to escape the many revolutions of their great Motherland.

And Shanghai—that Sodom, where sickness, sin and misery were so firmly ensconced—had yet received so much help from civilization in the form of money and pills that, even if never reformed, it could boast a clean and smiling façade.

Singapore, Hongkong and Shanghai—what feelings of sadness the mere sound of their names awakens in the heart of an old traveller in Eastern Asia. And Ilo-ilo, Kowloon, Manila and all the other beautiful places where we so often went ashore on adventure bound. Thank God for the sweetness of experience and the strength of memory!

I hear the brittle melody of bells from the China coast pagodas; I feel the wind's soft play in the palms of Trengganu, I watch the splendid display of colours in the sunset over Manila Bay; and I see the hospitable, friendly smile on the faces of the many who have handed me scented tea.

I am fond of dwelling on the first landing of my first cruise—when my eyes were big and round, my blood hot and my responsibility light. I was young and untried, and everything was great and new and wonderful. And I must have had fortune's gay feather in my helmet, for everywhere I found pretty little ears which were willing to listen to all I felt—and that was much!

I saw Singapore with two little princesses whose father was uncle to the King of Siam; they had a fellow feeling for me because their brother had been a Danish naval cadet. They showed me how the sticky resinous gum is made to run from the slender gum trees; they grilled strange fish for me in the natives' jungle huts, and climbed into the highest palm-tops like monkeys to giggle at my muscular helplessness. I stood them pink gin slings in John Little's famous bar, and enjoyed their supple grace under the humming punkahs on the Raffles' smooth dancing floor.

One night we drove down to the beach in light rickshaws to see the gentle waves of the Java and China Seas throw themselves into each other's arms, and to count the jewels in the glittering diadem of the Southern Cross. We had with us the whole of the band from the Raffles, a party of brown natives who played as in a dream, as though drawing every note out of the black tropical night. To seaward, the rustle of the flying fish sounded like mermaids' love-lorn sighing, while from the jungle came the mysterious noises of hunting and hunted beasts, and the sky sprinkled a rain of shooting stars over our heads. . . .

We sail through the China Sea and cruise among the many small islands, rich in adventure, of the Sulo Sea. In the dark tropical nights the phosphorescence glitters like gold spangles along the ship's sides ; at dawn the shining porpoises tumble in the rushing coolness of our wake, and school after school of silvery flying fish fly in a long gliding sweep over the sea's mirror-calm surface.

Many of the palm-clad coral islands we glide past are so flat that at a distance they look like slender palm-bunches stuck down in the sea ; on others small huts built of boughs, and waving people, are seen ; and among the islands cruise long narrow outrigger boats with huge sails, manned by smiling naked crews.

Slowly and cautiously our ship works her way in through the long, dangerous entrance to the sheltered anchorage of Ilo-ilo. The entrance is so narrow and the thickly-wooded slopes so steep and high, that we sometimes feel as if we were sailing right through the virgin forest itself. Straight cedar trees grow high above the ship's masts ; we glide among ebony trees, mahogany, papaja and shady fern trees, round whose trunks wild epiphytes and orchids clamber.

At last we see light ahead and we drop anchor in the natural harbour of Ilo-ilo, where the great Magellan once sought refuge.

We are received by a smiling deputation, which hurries through the legal inspection to bid us welcome the more eagerly. They are Uncle Sam's representatives in this remote paradise. They are all clad in uniforms with padded shoulders, perfectly American, but their colour is that of the most delicious café au lait, their eyes are quiet and gentle, and they bear themselves like Spanish grandees ; of course they all talk American with a broad Hollywood accent, but their talk is full of polite Spanish phrases whose American equivalents they have presumably sought for in vain in school-books and dictionaries.

I went ashore with the local quarantine doctor, who insisted on introducing me into the American club at Ilo-ilo. The quay is fine, new and clean, and reminds one of many other American quays. It is bordered by white plastered houses, which contain the local offices of the New York City Bank, American Express Company, Standard Oil, and all the rest of the dollar firms which have conquered the world.

But the whole of this American business street is only a thin façade along the sea-front, erected to please and deceive the rich, lazy tourist. Behind the quay is hidden the real Ilo-ilo, the old town which was founded by Spanish pirates, built by Catholic monks, and carried through centuries of prosperity by their descendants intermarried with the native Filipinos.

We turned off through streets bounded by walled gardens, past Catholic churches built centuries ago by Spanish architects, and wound our way forward to the promised American club. There are certainly not many Americans who have set foot in this club, and its members, from a racial standpoint, satisfied absolutely none of the usual requirements for admission to the " White " clubs of the East ; but I think of all clubs it is the one to which I would most like to belong. There was neither bar nor billiard-room ; I saw hardly one pure white member, and membership was emphatically not restricted to males.

My new-found doctor friend and his companions placed me

at a round marble table which was soon groaning under a load of cool drinks. The whole company was more or less " coloured ", but they did their utmost to make me feel at home. I was loudly hailed with " Hello, old boy ", slapped on the shoulder and treated to other expressions of American heartiness, but it was difficult to follow the lively gesticulations, and there was evidently a good deal that was more easily expressed in Spanish than in the new mother tongue.

I let them talk and gesticulate and made myself as small and inconspicuous as possible, for the door leading into the next room stood ajar, and through the chink I could hear insinuating song and the happy chatter of cheerful girls. I rose and stretched myself under the humming punkah without apparently attracting the attention of those at my table. Then I slipped over to the door, and great was my joy.

In the adjoining room a dozen dusky beauties were dancing a figure dance in which Spanish grace and Philippine charm received full expression. They all had raven hair and big dark eyes, while their colour varied between the palest white and the darkest café au lait. Most of them were wearing old Spanish dresses with short transparent puffed sleeves, high coiffures and mantillas with large tortoiseshell combs, but a few had long dangling plaits, bare brown shoulders, and all the jungle's wildness in their supple movements and burning eyes. They all abandoned themselves completely to the dance, humming its tune with heads thrown back ; their eyes were bright and their lips moist, and one could follow the play of every muscle under the long flimsy dresses.

My table companions' high-pitched laughter suddenly broke the spell. They had once more become a hundred per cent. Yankee, and were behaving in perfect accordance with the Hollywood etiquette they had learned from the white screen. Shouting and grinning they dragged me into the dancing room, where our entrance caused the immediate disappearance of naturalness and beauty. The bewitching creatures of a moment before stood like a crowd of scared, insipid schoolgirls and cast sidelong glances at the stranger under their long velvety eyelashes. One of the leading spirits shouted to the girls some noisy rigmarole in Spanish—I suppose he said they must now do the American club honour, or something of that kind ; after which he flung the most delicious of the goddesses into my arms, while one of his companions set the gramophone going. I don't know what we danced, but she swayed like a Dryad, and the sugary atmosphere of " Come with me to Moon Bay " was transformed into the most delightful romance.

Perhaps my eager desire was to be read in my face, and perhaps they were anxious to impress the charms of Ilo-ilo upon me as strongly as possible ; for all the rest of the time till the *Hector's* siren summoned all aboard next morning, I had little Rositta at my side to point them out to me.

We drove through the streets of the old town in a two-wheeled *calesa*, and I felt myself carried away to Spain—and to a past century. Everywhere Spanish was spoken ; the streets had Spanish names ; churches, gardens and walls were Spanish, and the young women in their mantillas and old Spanish dresses swayed at the hips as softly as the girls of Valencia.

We came out of the town and went on between green rice and sugar plantations to the edge of the wood, where we plucked bananas from their clusters and shook coconuts from the palm-tops to enjoy their cool milk.

The sun went down while we were catching striped and speckled fish in the waters of a lagoon, and when at last we drove home, all the stars of the southern sky were twinkling over our heads. It was an incomparably sweet, exotic night ! The Southern Cross stood high in all its beauty ; from an old church we heard the voices of monks singing mass ; the crickets ground out their shrill music, and the garden was full of the scents of jasmine and flame flowers.

Another three days' sail across the China Sea, and we sighted Hongkong. The sun was setting as we dropped anchor in

the narrow strait between the " Valley of the Scented Waters "
and the " Nine Dragons ".

The island's pyramid-shaped rock rose as a dark silhouette against the myriads of stars of the limpid Chinese sky. Then the lights were lit along the quay, and as by the stroke of an enchanter's wand, all the cupolas burst into illumination along the winding road that leads to the top of the cliff—and slowly, one by one, the dark space between the serpentine road and the star-strewn sky was filled with glittering points of light.

Next day I went ashore at Hongkong. I wandered through bazaars that teemed with life, and imbibed the indescribable, fascinating sounds and scents of China. I came out on the broad white square before the Victoria Club, where the famous Queen and other great personages of the Empire look proudly from their marble pedestals.

Down by the quay at Kowloon lay a small octagonal pavilion, where delights of many kinds could be bought cheaply. Every evening on my way home I looked in to buy an armful of lovely carnations which I placed in my sultry little hotel bedroom. The pavilion was owned by an old Chinese, Ah Lin, whose youngest wife, number five, was only twenty-four. Ah Lin was a smart chap, and his five wives were not there for his pleasure only, but had to make silk embroidery and other things which he sold in his little flower shop. To look after his business he had obtained from an English mission station a girl of seventeen called Julia. Her mother, a Chinese prostitute, had handed her new-born child over to the mission and disappeared from her life forthwith. Julia's father was an unknown English sailor who had landed at Hongkong eighteen years before. The baby had received the name Julia at the mission station, and she herself had christened the unknown sailor Mr Gill, and that was how she had become Miss Julia Gill.

The whole of Julia's life had been spent at the mission station among none but good people, till she had suddenly fallen into the hands of this unscrupulous, avaricious Chinese. In the evenings drunken sailors came to the pavilion to buy tobacco, and from their lips Julia heard words of whose existence she had previously had no idea. Sometimes the customers' behaviour was such that only fear of her Chinese master kept her from running away altogether.

She was pretty, was little Julia; she possessed all the luxuriant beauty and charming unaffectedness which characterize so many Eurasian girls when they get outside the walls of a mission station; and I enjoyed our daily tête-à-tête over the buying of flowers. One day, when she was reaching for a specially beautiful flower for my bouquet, she knocked over a shelf of small porcelain figures, and all of them were broken. She began to sob at the thought of the consequences when her old Chinese found out, and her fear was so heart-rending that, from an impulse of pure compassion, I bought all the broken figures.

Two days later, when I was due to continue my journey northward, Julia stood on the quay to bid me farewell. When at last I had to tear myself away, she pressed five large, bright red carnations into my hands, and while all those round us shouted and hallooed as people seeing others off are accustomed to do, she whispered in my ear : " And when you come back, I shall never be careless again."

The good-bye was over, and we were gliding out into the driving morning mists of Hongkong Bay. Now and then the fairylike veil of mist was pierced for an instant, and we caught a glimpse of the loveliest little pictures—palm-clad mountain slopes with the palaces of the Hongkong people, as white as marble, heaving sampans with huge blood-red sails—and then the sun broke through and cast a long strip of gold over the still surface. The glittering path ran right to the ship's side, so near that I could have jumped down on to it, and continued far away, into infinity. . . .

I sat and gave memory and imagination combined free play. Imagination told me that the path of gold, cast by the sun over the calm surface of the China Sea, led straight to the object of our desires. My objectives were many and great—but the first was called Shanghai.

FROM SHANGHAI TO PEKING

I AM sitting on board one of the China Steam Navigation coasting vessels, gazing out over the blue shining mirror of the China Sea. There is not a breath of wind, the air quivers with heat, and the sea-birds which follow eternally in the ship's wake doze torpidly on their great outspread wings. The passengers have scattered to their respective cabins, and the native crew lie curled up in shady corners to enjoy their siesta. In the distance a coast is dimly visible, so devoid of landmarks that it seems to be the same section of horizon which we have left astern.

But for the old China missionary at my side the land ahead holds so many memories that they must be told. He tells me stories of his long life in the Chinese mission field—and the grey, negative horizon of China becomes alive with exotic pictures.

I see grey water buffaloes dragging primitive wooden ploughs through the rich soil of Kwangtung; perspiring coolies at work in irrigated rice-fields; thousands of busy hands making the loveliest lace in the province of Fukien; and broad thickets of flowering mulberry trees.

Of an evening, when we were not sitting in dumb contemplation of the stars of heaven or the sea's glittering phosphorescence we told each other about ourselves.

He had when quite young felt a call to preach God's word and gospel to China's millions of heathen, and in the past thirty-six years he had visited all the most suffering provinces in the mighty Central Empire. But his fondest memories were of his young days, when he and two others of his creed opened the Methodist Mission, now so powerful, on Hainan, the " Island of Palms ". But he was unwilling to give himself and the two comrades of his youth all the credit for the fact that the natives on Hainan now had schools, hospitals and Christian churches ; for they, the first pioneers of the Methodist Mission, had themselves had a predecessor, a mighty champion of the Lord, who had lived and worked on the island in the last eighteen years of his life.

This man, whose name was Carl C. Jeremiassen, had been fantastically rich when he came to the island, but he had done so much good with his money that when he died in 1901 he owned nothing. The whole of his fortune had been spent in alleviating the natives' hardships. But Jeremiassen had at the same time achieved something in many other fields.

When the three pioneers of the Methodist Mission came to the Island of Palms, they had found many small Christian communities, mainly among the wild volcanic mountains in the interior of the island. The mountain people were the remnants of the island's original population, and were very different in race, manner of life, and speech from the Chinese who lived along the coast.

In Jeremiassen's old house the three Methodist missionaries had found a quantity of material which was of great use to them in their work. They found among other things a carefully drawn map of the island, and the manuscripts for both a dictionary and a grammar of the mountain people's peculiar speech. All this material, laboriously prepared by Jeremiassen, the Methodist missionaries had had published, and it was still of inestimable value to the many American missionaries on the island.

When I found out that Jeremiassen was a Dane, I naturally

pricked up my ears, and I began to pump the American for information as to how my countryman had come to the Island of Palms and in what circumstances he had died. But the American missionary was not interested in Jeremiassen except as regarded that part of his work which had been of profit to the mission, and I understood that his evangelistic methods had not been entirely approved. Nor was it a good sign, the missionary thought, that on the walls of several of the island's heathen temples paintings and drawings were to be found depicting a strongly-built white man with a big, fair beard. These were presumed to represent my countryman ; but a good Christian would not wish to live his life in such a way as to be exalted to a divinity by the natives.

My fellow-passenger told me that Jeremiassen had certainly been employed in the China Customs service before he began his work on the Island of Palms, and went on to explain how God's word ought to be conveyed to the natives. But I found it impossible to follow him, for I could not detach my thoughts from the solitary Dane. He must have been a great personality, for otherwise he could not have converted bloodthirsty savages into gentle Christians, and still less, after his death, could he have figured as a mighty divinity among savage heathens . . .

On the third day of the voyage the blue China Sea assumes a yellowish hue, and on the fourth morning the sea is so mud-coloured that a silver coin disappears the instant it strikes the surface.

We take a pilot on board and pass between countless mudbanks with flat, luxuriant verges, and we are surrounded by swarming noisy life. Big deep-laden junks glide slowly past us under huge blood-red sails. With their towering poops they look like Phœnician sailing-ships ; but the great eyes painted on the bows and the long antennæ at the mast-tops leave no doubt that the Land of Dragons is their home.

Among the dignified junks shoot hundreds of small sampans. The little light boats are under water to the rails beneath the weight of cargo of all kinds, and under the awning forward are the owner, his family and all his worldly goods. A thin feather of smoke rises from an open galley; the craft is alive with naked babies and speckled hens. The whole ship's company shriek and yell to encourage the child who is working their boat sinuously forward, and to jeer at and curse the rowers in all the other boats which are ceaselessly getting in the way.

The sampans are the gipsies of the river. All the swarming families on board the many small boats are born and do their work on the muddy water of the river, and many of them die without ever having set foot on China's yellow soil.

On both sides of the majestic river the Chinese fields extend—green and fertile and covered with small barrows, clay-lined huts, black pigs, willow-trees and children, children everywhere. We turn into the Yangtse.

The river takes a bend, and right in the middle of the curve Shanghai appears behind a forest of masts, sails and chimneys. First the twenty stories of the huge Cathay Hotel are seen, then the pointed black tower of Sassoon House, the monstrous cupolas of the Hongkong and Shanghai Bank, and the whole row of white buildings that constitute the ugliest and most imposing city horizon in the world.

We cover the last few miles of the journey in a little steam launch, low in the greasy yellow water, and we shoot past a navy of merchant ships representing a dozen different nations, and an armada of grey armoured giants that watch over the Great Powers' interests in China.

Then the launch reaches the Bund, and I go ashore at Shanghai.

In the next few days I see the " city with seven lives ", and after a week I am overpowered by exotic impressions. There is no doubt that Shanghai, for all its façade of sky-scrapers, and despite its arrogant, triumphant airs of wealth and power, is a Chinese city.

A curiously heterogeneous traffic presses ceaselessly through the crooked lanes and streets. The shining black motor-cars of the Taipans[1] and Compradors[2] are swallowed up in the crowd of primitive carts, wheelbarrows and rickshaws. I have to push and elbow my way forward through a ceaselessly flowing stream of blue-clad Asiatics; everywhere I see the thousands of beardless countenances that seem to be so many facets of one single countenance, enormous and inscrutable.

Down on the Bund the perspiring harbour coolies chant their gloomy working song, the same notes the whole day long—Hai-yo! Hai-yo! Hundreds of thousands of coolies sing and sweat the whole day long, day after day.

A stone's throw from the sky-scrapers on the Bund I pass workshops and shops, open to the street, and see how all the Chinaman's necessaries of life are made. Twenty young men bend their grey faces over sewing machines; half a dozen short-sighted young girls stare themselves blind in embroidering artistic patterns; and coppersmiths swing heavy hammers with thin, sinewy arms. In the medicine shop the strangest things are on show. Miracle-working roots, shaped like human beings, stick up out of neat little boxes; dried seeds lie heaped in piles; healing herbs, fishes' bladders and thousands of other things lie wrapped up in the most curious packings.

And while I went about, gazing at the swarming life of Shanghai, my thoughts continually returned to my solitary countryman who was the first of all to preach the gospel to the natives of Hainan. Where had he come from, and how did it happen that he landed on the remote Island of Palms? The old missionary had told me that Jeremiassen had certainly been employed in the China Customs service before he became an evangelist, so perhaps I could satisfy my curiosity at the China Customs head office here in Shanghai.

The only information in the archives of the Customs office was that Jeremiassen had belonged to the staff from 1878 to 1880. However, an old Chinese clerk was able to tell me that an old Scotsman was still living in Shanghai who in the

[1] Business chiefs.   [2] Chinese heads of staffs.

eighties and nineties had been captain of a lightship on the north coast of Hainan, so that he might have been in contact with Jeremiassen. I found MacGregor's name in the telephone book and went to the address, which was in the French concession of Shanghai.

The street was in an obscure part of the city, and the house proved to be a large tenement building, swarming with Chinese children. On the third floor I saw " MacGregor " on a door, and rang the bell. A pretty young Russian woman opened the door a few inches, and when she heard that I wanted to see Mr MacGregor, she introduced herself as Mrs MacGregor and asked me to wait for her husband, who was expected home soon. Her English vocabulary was very limited, and I was surprised that a man who had been a captain fifty years ago could possess so young and attractive a wife and inhabit a home so totally devoid of any trace of old Scotland.

My astonishment was increased when, an hour later, her husband appeared and proved to be a middle-aged Chinese half-caste. But his reply to my hesitating question, whether he had ever been captain of a lightship in the South China Sea, supplied the explanation : he was MacGregor junior, son of the captain of the lightship, and the latter now lived at 46 Rue de la Paix.

46 Rue de la Paix was a neat little house, bright with white-plastered walls and well-polished windows. This time the door was opened wide by a fat old Chinese woman, who assured me with a grin that she was the right Mrs MacGregor. Filled with suspicion and doubt, I followed her through a few pleasant rooms to a door before which a thick curtain hung. Her rather timid knock was answered by a few resounding Scottish oaths, on which she pushed me into the innermost room of the house.

There was no doubt that I had now found my man. Before an open fireplace sat a white-haired old sea-dog, his face bronzed and furrowed by tropic suns and typhoons ; his open shirt and turned-up sleeves disclosed the most delightful old-fashioned tattooing. On the wall behind his big armchair hung a faded old piece of cloth whose embroidered letters still announced " My home is my castle ". The same motto was clearly to be read in the keen watery-blue eyes which the old man turned on me as I entered. But as soon as I explained my errand his surly demeanour turned to gentleness, and I understood that I had touched a string it was pleasant to him to hear.

Yes, he had indeed known Jeremiassen, and he had never known a better man. And so he gave me his testimony, which largely corresponded to my expectations.

Jeremiassen was not one of those people who like talking about themselves—Captain MacGregor declared emphatically —but his name was so well known in the good old days that all who had lived in those times must necessarily have heard fragments of his strange history. No one knew when Jeremiassen had come to China, but everyone knew that his home country was Denmark and that at the end of the seventies he had appeared in the South China Sea, where he soon made himself notorious as the most daring of the many pirates who at that time played havoc in those waters. In 1879 lawlessness in the China Sea had become so general that it threatened to block completely the important trade routes to Canton, and the viceroy in the Canton area, who was responsible for the maintenance of peace and order in that part of the world, received serious threats from the highest authority in distant Peking.

As a last resource to save his threatened position, he determined to buy Jeremiassen over to his side, so that the former pirate might co-operate in making war on all the corsairs with whom the authorities were unable to cope. Jeremiassen accepted the viceroy's offer, and, equipped with a well-armed fast gunboat, started a campaign against his former fellow-pirates. Countless were the battles he fought, many the prizes he made, and so decisive were his victories that the China Sea in the course of a few years was transformed into a peaceful stretch of water.

Jeremiassen had in a short time earned a large fortune, first as a pirate and then in fighting the pirates, and if he had been a Chinese, he might have returned to his first profession so as to be in a position to repeat the profitable manœuvre. But Jeremiassen was only a young Dane whose exciting adventures had gone to his head. Now he had grown a few years older, the new had become old and the intoxication was passing off; and so he began his second life, not so much because he regretted the life he had lived previously, but from a desire to do good with the fortune he had acquired.

He had first gone as a pupil to a well-known mission doctor, who at that time was working in Canton; and then he had loaded his old pirate ship with provisions, medical stores and Bibles for a last cruise across the China Sea.

In 1881 he landed on the Island of Palms, where he at once set about his self-appointed task as an evangelist. As Jeremiassen felt a call to missionary work more among the savage natives in the interior of the island than among the tame Chinese who lived along the coast, he had first to learn their language, and as there were no dictionaries or grammars to which he could have recourse, he had himself laboriously compiled such works. With the passage of years he had become rather a kind of popular leader and sage than a preacher of God's Word to the natives, and he had been as welcome a guest in the savages' huts as in the Christian communities round the little chapels he himself had built.

When in 1901 he disappeared, the Chinese down on the coast maintained that he had been drowned when out sailing in the China Sea. But the mountain people knew better. Three of them had with their own eyes seen him ascend the highest peak of the island and step from its summit right into the white mist of the highlands.

Thus it had happened that the Dane Jeremiassen, who had once been a devastating pirate and ruthless freebooter, who had written learned school-books in a hitherto unknown language and built the first evangelical chapels on remote Hainan, was after his death exalted to a divinity by the savage mountain people of the Island of Palms.

I spent a long afternoon in old MacGregor's company, and he told me of all his meetings with Jeremiassen and related numerous incidents which illustrated my countryman's many rare qualities. There was no question that these memories, along with his recollections of the distant home he had left more than sixty years before and had never seen again, composed a substantial part of the old Scotsman's interest in life.

Before I left him he growled, with a hint of bitter envy in his voice : " Well, I've got stuck here and I've never got any farther, because I've had a Chinese wife tied round my neck. My son's more Chinese than white, his wife is a Siberian dancer, and their children are regular niggers. That's what the proud Clan MacGregor has come to in China. . . . Jeremiassen became both god and king, but he earned it honourably."

FROM SHANGHAI TO PEKING

The following day I left Shanghai and its swarming business life, and three days later I arrived in China's old imperial city, whence many roads lead out over the far-flung adventure-world of Central Asia.

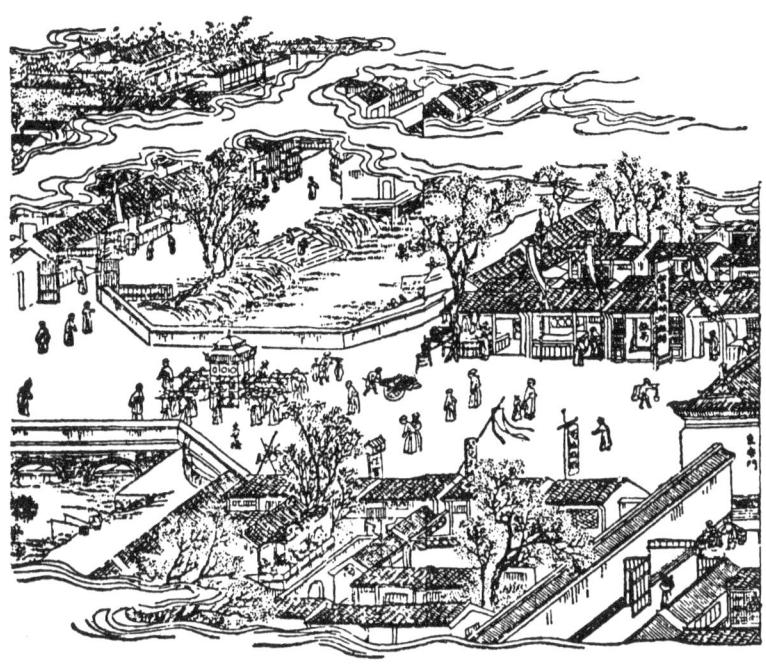

THE GIRL WHO PAINTED A FAN

AFTER a four-days' railway journey through dust and heat I reached Peking late in the afternoon. It was long ago that I last visited the old imperial city, but everything was unchanged. The grinning khaki-clad porters in front of the Water Gate took careful charge of my luggage; Wu came running to offer his lacquered rickshaw with as much certainty of acceptance as if he was meeting me by appointment, and the stout doorkeeper outside the Wagon Lits Hotel even remembered my Danish name.

Peking was in those days the world's most conservative city, and there was an atmosphere of changelessness about everything in the stately hotel. Everywhere I came upon old acquaintances; there were delighted welcomes and cheerful smiles, and when I raised my glass to congratulate myself on my lot, the dining-room's Russian orchestra struck up a tune which in old days had a permanent place on my musical list of desiderata.

Well fed and elated with wine, I sailed out through the swing doors to take my place in the lantern-hung rickshaw of the patiently waiting Wu. I let him take me where he liked —through the asphalt streets of the Legation quarter and into the narrow crooked lanes of the Chinese city.

It was the first cool evening of the summer, and I enjoyed the curious rocking motion which was communicated from Wu's running body, through the long supple shafts of the rickshaw, to my comfortable seat. Everywhere were swarms of cheerful, happy Chinese, waving striped lanterns and exchanging lively greetings, and from the huge acacias of the many gardens rose the strangest waves of sound from millions of chirping crickets.

At ten o'clock I ascended by the lift through the great building of the modern Hotel de Peking to watch the evening's festivities from the high roof garden. Up there it was pleasant and cool. In the centre of the roof there was dancing to soft insinuating music from a Hawaiian orchestra. Most of the dancers were young Chinese, belonging to the aristocracy and intellectual circles of Peking.

The young girls were full of conscious charm with their tall slender figures, graceful movements and tasteful dress. They looked like the daintiest porcelain figures in their long narrow brocade dresses, which descended respectably to their ankles and had modestly high collars, but were daringly slit up the sides high above the knee. White jessamine flowers flung their scent from the girls' coal-black locks, the dim lantern light of the roof garden played on their shining silk legs and worked patterns and shifting colours on the crackling brocade robes.

I sat and enjoyed the time and the place from my solitary table amid surroundings that were so dear to me. The large full moon, with her myriad train of glittering stars, cast a magic light over the open roofs of the imperial city with their light green, fiery yellow and cobalt blue stones. Everywhere coloured lanterns were swung, and the sound of thousands of voices rose like a sacrificial song to the night's great giver of light.

I was still sitting there when the moon with her train of stars grew pale before the light of the coming day, and was not awakened from my dreams till Hsi-pei feng, the earliest breeze of morning, came sweeping down from the Mongolian frontier mountains to the north-west, a freshening breath from the land of wide steppes and deep deserts.

Many of my journeys to Central Asia have started from Peking, and I have often spent in this old imperial city of Asia the intervals between my different journeys.

Peking—that incomparable city with its seductive mystery and its peculiar life ; that cultural centre of vanished days with its marble-white terraces and roofs gleaming with gold and blue ; where lotus-covered lakes surround the gracious pavilions of the " ten thousand ages ", and wind-blown, twisted cypress groves stand darkly on guard round altars, whence the chanting, ringing and roaring of the temples proclaim the faith and superstition of all Asia.

Peking ! the Tartar city with the old-fashioned life of its narrow lanes, whose inhabitants, fast bound in place and time, still listen to story-tellers' tales of the " five claps of thunder " and to the old songs of blind troubadours.

One of the many songs that has become current among the inhabitants of the *hutung*,[1] who still sing it, has the following opening verse :

> In a graceful pavilion, between poplar and willow,
> in the western part of Peking city,
> sits Bai Djyn-ying,
> a lovely Chinese girl, who can paint with colours.
> This beauty—nineteen winters old—
> strives not to betray her longing.
> Her lover is far away,
> and the fourth month is near.

[1] *Hutungs* are the narrow winding lanes which lie between the main thoroughfares of Peking.

THE GIRL WHO PAINTED A FAN

I had my Peking home for many years under the same poplars and willows which overshadow young Miss Bai's pavilion. This place was called Feng Chia Yuan, "Mr Feng's Park", and a Mr Feng was always owner of the houses and the garden, which until a short time ago I almost regarded as my own property.

It was Lenox Simpson who first took me to Feng Chia Yuan, and it was also he who installed me as ruler over the Feng family's forsaken heritage and over the old servant families who watched over this idyllic place while loyally awaiting the rightful owner's return.

I then understood from Simpson that the Mr Feng who was called by the servants of the house " the young master's son " was a man of sixty. " The young master's son " was a half-caste. He had been born and had grown up in one of the Mediterranean countries. Only once, shortly after his Chinese father's death, had he come to Peking to see the family property of which his father had so often spoken. But his and his French mother's stay in Feng Chia Yuan had been short, for the sound of a wailing woman's voice, calling on the dead father and husband by name all through the nights, had so discomposed them that they had hurried back to their smiling Mediterranean coast as quickly as possible.

It was the same reason which deterred other Chinese from renting the Feng family's old house, and now Simpson wanted me to inhabit it when I was in Peking and so prevent it from being confiscated by the rapacious generals of modern times.

It was said, Simpson told me, that old Feng, the man whom the servants of the house called " the young master ", had in his early youth been expelled to Kashgaria. Thence he had succeeded in escaping over the mountains to India, and went on to France. Here he married the Frenchwoman, and he had never again seen his own country or the home of his fathers.

Simpson wanted to tell me a good deal more—something connected with the mysterious woman's wailing which made Feng Chia Yuan so dismal—but he was murdered before I could hear his story, and many years were to pass before I myself experienced what he had hinted at in 1925.

As the years went by, I won the old serving people's confidence more and more, and by putting together what I heard from them with the fragments of *hutung* superstition which I was now and again able to snap up, I gradually fathomed the mystery surrounding the old Chinese house I inhabited.

My garden was bounded to the north by a high wall, through which a " moon gate " led to the isolated regions which form the women's side of a high-class Chinese home. The red lacquered doors of this moon gate were only opened towards evening, when old Li went through my garden to make purchases for the following day in the *hutung* outside. Old Li was blind, but the changing scents from the many flower-beds led him safely along all the cunning twists and turns of the garden path.

No longer did beautiful women look down over the high balustrade of the pavilion ; all the old harem lay silent and deserted. Only on quiet nights a faded voice was heard from within singing an old song to guitar accompaniment. It was always the same song, the song which was so popular out in the *hutungs* of the Tartar city, the " song of the girl who painted a fan " :

> In the fourth month it is spring,
> the cold blast has gone.
> But Bai Djyn-ying sits lonely and forsaken.
> She hides her thoughts behind a fan.
> It is blinding white, and the frame red as blood.
> To lighten her thoughts, she paints them on the fan.
>
> First she paints Peking, with walls and canals,
> with its nine gates and nine outer cities in all their splendour,
> then she paints the Forbidden City
> with six courts and three palaces.
> Above the " hall of gold " the palace of the dawn appears,
> whence the Emperor's high officials look east and west.

And on the fifteenth of every month, when the full moon stood round and high in the Peking sky, the silence around Feng Chia Yuan was broken by a woman's wailing, so heart-rending that it filled the night with terror. The lamentations came from the isolated pavilion whence no one except silent, blind Li ever issued.

Out in the *hutungs* of Peking they said it was " eternal love " weeping for her lost loved one, and they sang, as tradition bade, the song of the nineteen-year-old Bai Djyn-ying, who lost her bridegroom on the very wedding night, but who always remained faithful to him and became the symbol of all womanly virtues.

In Feng Chia Yuan's narrow *hutung*, which winds about in such labyrinthine fashion that no motor-cars or other swift traffic can use it, all communication is still done by rickshaw or hand-cart, and as more and larger parts of Peking are modernized, it becomes a centre for all the old Peking life which is driven away by neon lights, the clatter of trams and the noise of wireless.

Here all the old Peking street traders assemble with their moveable shops and exchange " foreigners' fire " (matches), " the scent of still water " (lotus seeds and roots) and old " jade rice " (corn cobs). Here all traffic stops willingly and gladly to amuse itself yet again with the " man with the performing fleas ", or to seek advice from the " doctor of the old school " and the " astrologer who sees into the future ". They are all representatives of ancient guilds which have characterized Peking street life for centuries, and they all use regularly the same little songs and street cries which have appealed to countless generations of customers.

I have loved all these Peking sounds, so full of significance, and the breath of the living past which they brought into the old *hutungs* and the abandoned palaces of the imperial epoch.

When the sun has gone down behind the " western mountains ", and the twilight has hushed the hungry chorus of

crickets, I have sat in my old garden to listen and observe. And from my place under the tall acacia I have seen, through the open moon gate, the life of the *hutung* pass by in the light of the flickering oil lamps. All my neighbours and their households, who all day long have remained hidden behind bolt and bar, now come swarming out to enjoy the sociability of street life for one or two cool evening hours. And all the street traders and all the cheerful rascals come hurrying to satisfy the inhabitants' smallest wishes or needs. There are jokes and chatter, eating and laughter, and the air becomes full of incense and the smell of food.

They do all this partly just to have the pleasure of doing something, and when they have listened for a time to the blind singers and the story of " the five thunder-claps ", they withdraw to the seclusion of their respective Chinese homes. The gates are barred, and the evening market is at an end. Then nothing more is heard but the clash of the watchmen's castanets—some have a different ring from others—the piercing love songs of a few crickets, and the hushed note of the conch which announces a night service in one of the city's temples.

July 31, 1936, was my last night of full moon in Feng Chia Yuan. The noise of the *hutung* had died away, and the night was filled with expectant silence. It was the evening for the manifestation of " undying love " ; but I sat waiting in vain for the tortured weeping which had mystified and fascinated me for so many years. Only the loud chirping of a single cricket was heard—a cricket which had fulfilled its mission and was now singing its death song. Its chirping would soon stop, and a little noise, like the falling of a bird's egg from a nest, would announce the nocturnal musician's death.

Suddenly dragging steps were heard from the harem, a hesitating rattling on the heavy copper-work of the door, and two figures appeared in the round moon gate—a little shrunken woman hanging heavily in old Li's thin arms. He laid down his burden carefully against one of the stone lions which guarded the entrance to the harem. Then he went back and reappeared carrying an old-fashioned guitar.

I gazed fascinated into the old woman's face, which looked like a fantastic mask in the bluish sheen of the moonlight. I had never seen anything so furrowed and marked by time. It seemed unbelievable that those skeleton-like eye sockets could see, that that collapsed mouth could utter words, and that that shrunken mummy's head could still contain human thoughts.

Silent and motionless as the stone figure she was leaning against, strange and mysterious as the *hutung* legends themselves, she sat up against the darkness of the moon gate, the darkness which was " the undying love's " refuge from the world. From her thin hand hung an open fan, richly painted with scenes and symbols in exquisite colours.

Old Li fumbled with the guitar till he struck up a tune ; the painted fan rose slowly to follow the rhythm of the music ; the furrows and wrinkles of the face were twisted convulsively, then were smoothed out again and came to rest ; black eyes became visible behind a glittering veil of bright tears, and her feelings found expression in song, the song of " the girl who painted a fan " :

> Day and night the same thoughts,
> year after year the same longings ;
> tears run like autumn rain
> without ceasing down my cheeks.
>
> In the pond lotus flowers were seen dimly
> between the rushes on the bank.
> Ah, my friend was taken from me ;
> noble was he, without fault,
> tall and beautiful in body and soul.
> Never comes forgetfulness to me,
> and in eternal craving
> I must press my cheeks
> against the pillows, wet with tears.

I listened fascinated to the quavering song of the woman of 108, the ancient words and confidences, and I was carried resistlessly back to her time and world.

The huge stone beasts of the sarcophagi tramped heavily through the desolate *hutung*. The forsaken halls and empty courts of the Forbidden City were peopled with emperors and princes. Artists and warriors performed their tasks. Priests and eunuchs unveiled each other's intrigues, and little princesses and beautiful concubines disclosed their hearts' romances. The imprisoning walls of the garden disappeared in the darkness, the balcony over my head was filled with inquisitive little beauties, and the " symbol of undying love " by my side was transformed into a bride of nineteen watching for her lover.

The Emperor Tao Kwang sat on the Dragon Throne and ruled the Central Empire. The lovely Bai Djyn-ying, the Empress's demure maid of honour, was betrothed to the noblest page at court, and the astrologers had fixed the luckiest day for their wedding. The young page's father was Feng, the learned mandarin, whose family's ability and conspicuous loyalty for generations past had made it rich and powerful.

But a Manchu prince had cast his eyes on the young maid of honour ; her unconquerable virtue turned his longing into hateful desire, and when the mandarin Feng tried to defend the honour of his house, he received the silk cord which meant death. An imperial edict exiled the young page to remote Kashgaria.

The ancient home of the Feng family lay unprotected, without a master. Day after day the pleasure-loving young girls and concubines of the harem were lured out to the temptations of the *hutung*, the old women mourned themselves to death over the fate which had overtaken the house, and at last only Bai Djyn-ying was left, waiting faithfully with the old servant families for the return of the exiled one.

Year after year Bai Djyn-ying waited in her chaste bridal chamber. Her beauty faded, her bridal dress was worn out, but her love endured.

Four times it was announced from the Forbidden City that one Emperor was dead, long life to another, and at last China became a noisy republic. Poverty and hardship knocked at the gates of the Feng home, and old Li sold bit after bit of

the old park. Only Bai Djyn-ying's pavilion, and as much of the park as she could see with her eyes, stood untouched and unchanged as in the time of long ago in which she still lived.

Generation followed upon generation in Peking's palaces and huts. The song of " the girl who painted a fan " became

a memory of the past; Bai Djyn-ying was transformed into the legendary symbol of undying love whose cries of agony could be heard, on nights of full moon, rising from the old pavilion, but whose form no one could describe, because no one now living had seen it.

Slowly a new day began, and the noises of the dawn mingled with the old woman's words ; and when the first redness reached the lion by the moon gate, she had collapsed by its cold stone paws. Silently and indulgently old Li lifted her up to carry her to the bridal chamber in the pavilion. Then he came back to fetch her guitar and the fan, which had fallen from her powerless hand. It lay half open in the grass, showing the symbols of purity, faith and love.

A slight noise from the lawn told me that last night's cricket had finished its death song, and when the red lacquered door of the moon gate shut on old Li, I felt that the curtain had fallen at the end of a drama.

IN THE HEART OF JASAKTU LAND

WANG-YEH MIAO is one of the newest stations on the Taonan-Solon line, one of many links which in recent years have been laid down in a north-westerly direction from the Trans-Manchurian Railway. Wang-yeh Miao is, moreover, the important point from which Nan Sheng, the most southerly of the four provinces of Hsingan-Mongolia, is ruled.

There are a new and an old Wang-yeh Miao, but the old town is not so old that the oldest Jasaktu Mongols cannot remember when Chinese merchants built the first clay huts on the open steppe. Then came the Chinese colonists who ploughed the surrounding country, and in their wake followed the mandarins who exacted taxes for the generals interested in the Chinese colonization.

All the mandarins and most of the colonists and merchants fled back to their Chinese homes in the eventful days of 1932, when Manchuria became Manchukuo and Hsingan an autonomous state under Japanese protection, and the few who remain now declare that they are real " Manchukuo people ", who honour Japan and despise China.

The Chinese Wang-yeh Miao is already fading away into a memory which nobody troubles to preserve.

If one rides a few miles west from the mandarins' abandoned, collapsing official building, one comes to the new Wang-yeh Miao, which was born simultaneously with the foundation of the new State. It is a modern town with imposing buildings, factories with smoking chimneys, neat squares and green parks laid out round the great Modji-Yamen, the provincial government building. It is from this place that the inexorable decrees of the new system are issued, that propaganda offensives are planned and directed ; and to it is brought the wild, dirty, splendid youth of the steppes. After a few months' physical and mental polishing-up they walk about the streets wearing tight uniforms and white gloves. They smell of Japanese cleanliness, and they salute their many new superiors like young guardsmen. But their grin, uncouth and genial, has disappeared.

From the Modji-Yamen one can see and hear a still newer town a few miles away. It has no name, it is not marked on any accessible map, and the uninitiated person does not show too open an interest in it, for its houses look like barracks and its sounds are words of command, sirens and the clash of weapons. It is one of the great centres which form the backbone of the Japanese' dense chain of vigilant frontier guards in the west, and the place where all the fit men in the province are trained for the " great advance ".

The atmosphere which prevails in the Mongols' new town is very un-Mongolian. No meditating greybeards or gloomy prophets are to be found there. One sees almost entirely young men in uniform, and practically no women. Traffic in the streets and work in the offices are conducted at a feverish pace, and everywhere one comes upon impassable sentries, guarding secrets.

I had often entered Mongolia—over the Red frontier to the north, over the snowy peaks of the Himalaya and through the bandit-ridden Chinese frontier provinces—but never had the land of the nomads seemed so unapproachable as now. Here there was no chance of sneaking past sleeping mercenaries on a dark night or of tempering the authorities' severity with a good dinner.

But I wanted to get across that frontier, and I relied on the stars, which had given me a young Mongol's friendship. I had succeeded in making Dundurdjab an enthusiastic supporter of my plans. To him my journey in Mongolia meant that his unenlightened countrymen in the interior would be brought into contact with the outside world and modern knowledge, which he so uncritically admired.

With Dundurdjab I went to every place where he could have any influence, and my desire to break through the innumerable obstacles which blocked the road to the seductive desert could not have had a more effective advocate. When all suspicion and opposition had at last been overcome, I was nevertheless very despondent, for none of these helpful people, who were all new to the country, could put me on the track of anything I wanted to see. I was taken from place to place by enthusiastic young guides, who showed me schools, hospitals, and a quantity of statistics showing most conclusively all the progress which the country and people had made in the past five years. This was very interesting, but it was not what I had come all that long way to study.

Once or twice I got into conversation with old Puntsuk. He sat in state at a huge writing-table up in the Modji-Yamen itself, surrounded by hard-working young clerks. In his hand he held a large seal, which he mercilessly banged down on the many documents which were laid before him. The new regime had let Odei Wang's Keeper of the Seal retain his dignity in a new form, and the centuries-old seal of his tribe reposed continually, like a sceptre, in his powerful hands. He was still able to set the old seal of tradition on the many inventions of the new era.

One day he asked me if I should not soon have seen enough, and I confided to him that I had not yet had a glimpse of what I sought. He nodded, while his thoughtful eyes wandered along the rows of propaganda placards on the walls. Then he smiled at me, and his smile was like a promise.

Early one morning one of the maid-servants of my Japanese hostel came fluttering into my room full of some kind of important information, which she tried to impart to me in every possible way. The arms of her kimono swung like gaily-coloured windmill sails ; her bright almond eyes and the whole of her expressive childlike pantomime varied between concentrated eagerness and calculated impatience. I was awake in an instant and sat up, fully to enjoy this pleasant morning surprise. She was very pretty, as she stood there wrapped in her bright-coloured kimono and exuding all the mysterious scents of the Japanese morning toilet. But when I continued to give no sign of responding to her varied forms of exhortation, her patience gave way and she thrust her little fist right through one of the many paper window-panes.

She ought to have done this at once, for when she withdrew her kimono-clad arms I saw the cause of her excitement. In the yard outside sat a party of stern Mongols on horseback, and one of them was Puntsuk.

The little Japanese girl had come to this strange land from Japan's remote rice-fields only a few days before, and to her the wild horsemen clad in striped robes, with rattling silver sword-belts, were as exciting as the sight of real redskins in old-time war-paint would be to a North European confirmation candidate.

I ran out to offer the Mongols tea and tobacco; but Puntsuk looked coldly at the doll's-house hostel and the giggling Japanese girl. "We'll have tea up there," he said, waving his arm towards the misty blue line which marked the mountains to the north.

So off we rode, to the glorious music of hoof-beats, away from houses and smoking chimneys, passport control and whistling engines, to the regions where the dreariness of life is transformed into glowing romance. The sun rose and drove away the mists on the horizon. The purity of the morning was blended with the freshness of the autumn air. The horses had soft grass under their hooves, and we broke into an exhilarating gallop. Twittering larks rose and fell like arrows between sky and earth; the Mongols' faces, before so stern and shut, were transformed; they smiled on me like genial hosts. We were out on the Mongolian steppe.

I rode between Puntsuk and Sangerup. Both were old and worn by wind and weather, but with a youthful bearing and elasticity preserved by the daily training of an open-air life. They had both in their vanished youth been counsellors of Odei Wang, the dead Jasaktu chief, and for both of them the greatest joys in life were memories of those times.

Puntsuk had become a mournful philosopher, who observed with a certain interest, but with much suspicion, the new forces which so strongly influenced his world, and pitied the younger generation for all that it was losing. Sangerup, the troubadour, who had been Odei Wang's court singer, preserved all the old songs and ballads from those rich, proud and happy days which he had once sung by his late master's camp fire.

We reached the lower hills, and the horses' easy gallop became a laborious climb. At last I could no longer control my curiosity, and I asked Puntsuk where we were going and what the object of our ride was. For a long time he did not answer my question, but when at last our snorting horses reached the head of the pass, he halted our cavalcade and pointed out over the new view which revealed itself to us.

The hard contours of the mountains, like a sea turned to stone, flowed towards us from the remote horizon. I followed the direction of the Mongols' searching looks. A long pale streak ran like spilt milk between the mountains and ended far away, where a collection of gleaming white plaster buildings lay like a little white bouquet against the brick-red wall of a mountain side.

Puntsuk pointed towards the end of the pale cliff path. " We are going ", he said, " to Khatun Sume, the Princess's temple, but you will camp to-night in the heart of the Jasaktu country."

The Mongols' dreamy eyes wandered over the stupendous scenery around us, and the soft winds of the sunset hour were borne to us from the dusk of the valleys. Somewhere out in the strange silence the bark of a fox was heard, and the Mongols stiffened like hounds finding a scent. Then all was silent again, and the floating silhouette of a bird of prey glided over a sunlit mountain wall to vanish in the shadow of a cliff-top.

Puntsuk dismounted, and the others followed his example. For a while they sought among the stones which lay strewn in the pass. Then they approached a huge pyramid of stones which crowned the top of the pass, each man carrying a light-coloured stone in his hand. They murmured in chorus prayers and old magic formulas.

We stood before an *obo*, one of the largest I have ever seen—one of the old stone altars which are to be found in strange out-of-the-way places in Central Asia ; one of those mysterious places of sacrifice which are still secretly preserved, built of stone cast upon stone through many generations ; a home of mystery which has its roots in the origin of the people itself, and whose religious significance goes much farther back in time than any of the religions of the modern world.

From the stones of the pyramid old lances projected, from which ragged remnants of flat strips of silk, bearing inscriptions and animals, waved or rattled in the gusty mountain wind.

Suddenly Puntsuk gave a shout which awoke all the echoes of the desert, and the Mongols' stones rolled and rattled down the sides of the *obo* till they found their place and came to rest.

I was studying the Mongols' expressionless faces to catch the significance of the moment. Puntsuk read the inquiry in my eyes, and stepped back to me.

" We are standing ", he said, " at the Bayan Jeruke *obo*, the place of sacrifice in the mountain, within which the heart of the Jasaktu country beats. Our people have gone on campaigns to foreign countries, and we have followed our feeding herds on peaceful journeys to distant pastures, but the longing for our own land has always pursued us, till we pitched our tents again in the shelter of this mountain. Once, in the early days of our history, our great ancestor stood at this place, and here he felt the love of home awaken in his heart. The spirit of the Jeruke mountain laid hold upon him ; he gave the mountain his heart, and as a sign of this he laid the first stone on this altar. Since then no Jasaktu Mongol has failed to throw his stone, and the stones you saw us throw rolled over stones which were laid by our fathers and by their fathers before them, right from the day when the first stone marked the place of sacrifice.

"Splendid temples can arise at a mighty man's command to be consumed by time or an enemy's vengeance, but this our people's monument is a testimony from fathers to sons of our tribes' firm attachment to their homeland, and that will endure and grow so long as the Jasaktu Mongols are not cut off from their root."

The sun set, and the shadows of the mountains rose towards us from the depths below. Then the top of the pass was illuminated by the day's last ray of light, and the darkness closed round us. The horses and horsemen of the camp were turned to dark silhouettes, moving about amid creaking harness, rattling metal and old-world speech. It was an hour apart from time—a living reflection of a vanished time and a vanished world.

Puntsuk's horsemen collected dung, with which they lighted a noiseless fire. Then we gnawed the meat from the sheep-bones; Puntsuk lit his long pipe, Sangerup struck a few trial notes on his old string instrument, and the circle was formed round the evening fire under the high stars of Asia.

IN THE HEART OF JASAKTU LAND

The time had now come when the Mongols began to talk and sing without reserve, from their hearts, and I felt as if I, too, had taken root in the Jasaktu Mongols' earth. I heard this:

Khabto Khasar, eldest brother of the great Jenghiz Khan, stepped out of the fire " so broad-shouldered and slim-waisted that a dog could crawl under him when he slept on his side ". We followed him in our imagination, him and his host that was formed into the six *khorchin*, the " knife-sharp ", which covered the left flank of the conquering Mongol horde. From the Siberian snow wastes to China's rice-fields, through forest, steppe and desert, the unconquerable horsemen swept, intoxicated with victory and savage fury. Howls of terror rent the air, and we heard the slim arrows whistling past towards their doomed victims. A reek of human sweat, saddle-leather and enemy's blood mingled with the smoke from our fire.

And we came to the passes whence one looks out from the hardy land of the steppes over the wealth of China. There below us lay all the refined attractions which the Mongols had never yet tasted, and with a yell of lust the horde broke through the Wall of China and all other resistance to wallow in superfluity, women's beauty and power.

While the Mongol horde spread over the mighty Empire to enjoy its luxuries and rule its millions, we turned with Khabto Khasar and his " knife-sharp " men on a silent ride northward through Jehol's smiling alternation of deciduous woods, steppe and mountains, into the dark forests of Manchuria and back to the camp by the Bayan Jeruke *obo*, where Khabto Khasar had once felt a great peace lay hold upon his heart, like a soft fetter binding his restless soul to the earth he trod and to the beauty of nature he saw around him. . . .

Puntsuk had stayed his narrative in its flight over time and distance.

The camp fire lit up the circle of Tartars, sitting bent forward, and their listening faces. It was as though they were slowly waking up to the present day.

A man threw fresh dung on the fire. The bones on the old lances of the *obo* rattled, and Puntsuk knocked the ashes from his burned out pipe. Then he turned to me :

" Thirty-two generations of our people, with their chiefs of Khabto Khasar's race, have since that day stood here, understanding and humble. Now our young men are following new roads : they have found a new path, they say, that of the New Time, and they seldom come here to lay their stones on their fathers' stones. Perhaps the last stone will soon have been laid on the Bayan Jeruke *obo*."

These were Puntsuk's last words for that day, and as I lay in my sleeping-bag, these words, and all that they expressed, long occupied my thoughts.

The Mongols slept.

The moonlight out on the pass fell upon a white stone, which continually kept my thoughts awake. Every time I was on the verge of sleep, it shone out afresh, as full of visions and fantasies as a magician's crystal ball.

At last I got up and, obeying an impulse I could neither analyse nor resist, laid the stone in its place among the thousands of stones of the Bayan Jeruke *obo*.

And then I too fell asleep.

THE PRINCESS'S TEMPLE

ONE wakes early in the high mountain air of the Jasaktu country, and one is wide awake at once. The light atmosphere fills one with the liveliness and keenness of youth and the virgin purity of Nature clears the dusty corners of one's civilized soul.

We rubbed our eyes in the cold pearly rain of the morning dew, stretched our rested limbs in the first rays of the sun, and hastened to strike camp that we might ride on to meet the new day's adventures.

My Mongolian travelling companions were full of activity. The embers of the night before were blown up into flames, on which the round copper pot was soon chattering merrily, and when we had drunk masses of spiced compressed tea, the horses were caught and we started for our new destination.

The narrow path which showed us the way twisted and wound down into the narrow canyons, along babbling streams and over mountain passes, whence new views revealed themselves. Sometimes patches of colour which were herds of cattle sprang up from the lush depths of the green valleys, and young shepherds, watching over white sheep from high vantage points, sped us on our way with cheerful pipings.

As we went on, other narrow mountain paths joined our route, and at one of these points three young horsemen were waiting for us. On seeing them my companions dismounted, and we approached slowly on foot. Puntsuk and his men fell on the right knee and, with the right hand pressed to the ground, said : "*Amorgan sain, mendu sain, nojon*" (May the health of thy body and the peace of thy soul be preserved, O chief !).

I looked closely at the one of the three Mongols to whom this greeting was addressed. His slim figure swayed gracefully in the saddle with the capers of his impatient steed, while his smiling eyes curiously examined my strange face. His blue silk coat was of Mongolian cut, but the high plain riding boots and the grey felt hat on his raven hair were Western. His whole bearing, and the dignified friendliness with which he responded to the humble greeting of the others, showed that he was one of the great men of those parts ; but there was nothing to show whether he was one of the leaders of the new regime or an old-time chief. He could have been either.

Behind him were two Tartar hunters, men overflowing with vital energy. They wore fur-edged caps and their hair in long plaits ; one of them had a long bow hung at his side, and from the quiver on his back a bundle of feathered arrows stuck out like a huge fan. Their keen hunter's eyes were aslant, their faces bronzed by the burning sun of the mountains, and their teeth white and shining from much tearing of half-raw meat. Two splendidly natural specimens in these surroundings.

We joined forces and continued our journey. Our talk was inspired by our surroundings. Once the young prince rode up to my side for an exchange of courteous questions and answers. His name was Lamadjab, and he promised me, when I should continue my journey, such support as only a man with authority could give.

THE PRINCESS'S TEMPLE

Every time we reached a new pass, the goal of our journey had come nearer, and when the sun sank towards the western horizon, we could distinguish the red mural ornaments and the gilded figures on the roof of Khatun Sume, " the Princess's temple ".

We reached a broad grassy valley, cut by a blue mountain stream, and on the other side of it lay the little sanctuary stuck fast to the mountain side like a swallow's nest.

A party of men came up from the temple to meet us. Most of them were *harhung* (laymen) of the hunter type, but two of them were dressed in orange monk's robes. They all gave Lamadjab the humble greeting due to a chieftain, and while the hunters took charge of our horses, we followed the monks through the skilfully carved and painted portals of the temple, across the worn, grass-edged stones of the temple court and into the large guest-house. In the guest hall we were placed upon an oblong dais, where embroidered mats and back supports of different heights covered with magnificent rugs indicated the guests' places in accordance with their rank. A dim light entered through the painted paper window-panes and slowly revealed the details of the room. I wondered from what distant regions the heavy, worm-eaten roof-beams had been brought to these treeless mountains, and I studied the smoke-blackened wooden panelling, divided into octagonal fields, of the walls and roof. In each field a small picture had once been painted, and in the fantastic details of each picture the same light, delicate form appeared. In some of the pictures the artist's golden colours still shone out, but in most of them one could only faintly trace the lines of the colour scheme under the incrustation of centuries.

We inhaled the aroma of tea and exchanged conventional improvised trivialities. We were at our destination for that day, Puntsuk had said, but the atmosphere in the room suggested that the event of the day was still to come.

An old hunter appeared in the doorway and bent his knee

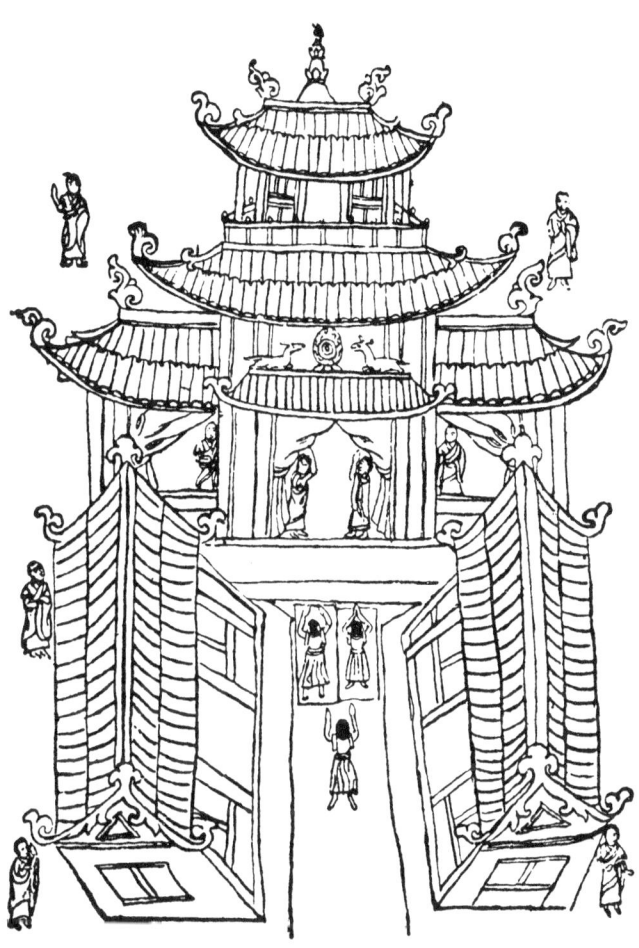

as he addressed Lamadjab. " My lord," he said, " everything is ready, and we await you."

Lamadjab sprang up and placed on his head the ceremonial headdress that was handed to him, and we followed him out into the little courtyard between the temples.

Here twelve hunters stood, drawn up facing the one of the four buildings which formed the north side of the courtyard.

THE PRINCESS'S TEMPLE

They were wearing old-time Manchurian ceremonial dresses, and held large silver-mounted sacrificial dishes on the palms of their extended hands. The offerings were rice, fruit, meat and other kinds of food, and over them blue *hadaks* (silk ribbons) were laid. Then the great doors of the temple were slowly opened, and mournful temple music and the smell of incense were wafted out to us.

Lamadjab, followed by the twelve hunters bearing the offerings, strode slowly into the dark mysterious interior of the temple, and passed between the red pillars of the central gangway to the back, where the light from the uncovered oil wicks of seven candelabra contended with the darkness in the great cavern. Old temple banners and golden gods became visible and disappeared again in the flickering light of the oil wicks. The back of the altar table consisted of a glass wall, which reflected the gold gleam of a pagoda three feet high.

Somewhere out in the darkness the great temple drums set up a deafening noise as Lamadjab stepped into the circle of light from the altar and threw himself down nine times with his forehead to the ground in the direction of the golden pagoda. One by one the twelve hunters carried their sacrificial dishes forward to Lamadjab, who lifted them reverently to his forehead and then laid them on the altar table. Puntsuk, Sangerup and the rest of the Mongols advanced to the altar, which they hung with blue ceremonial ribbons, and at an invisible sign they all fell down with their faces to the earth. This they did nine times in a deep *kowtow*, while the long temple horns wailed like strange wild beasts. Then the sacrificers withdrew from the circle of light round the altar, and the noise of the horns was silenced. The dull mumbling of the officiating priests was heard from the outer parts of the hall, and the tinkling of the temple bells at the roof corners sounded through the open doors.

We were back in the guest hall. Servants came bearing dishes loaded with mutton, and we satisfied our hunger. Then came the scented cups of tea, and a large copper dish filled with smouldering embers was placed on the *kang*. One by one we descended from the uncomfortable raised seats and crept together round the warm chafing-dish ; we drank tea and followed the clouds of smoke from the pipes as they hovered capriciously through the room.

The day was over, and a new evening was at hand, one of those long evenings which enable one to think over the fresh events of the day, get them into perspective and understand them.

I sat for a long time staring through the smoke from the pipes and the chafing-dish at the many small paintings on the roof, and I began to trace a connected mosaic illustrating the life of a high-born Oriental woman from her conception to the glories of heaven.

The twelve hunters had come and had lain down on the outer edge of the circle of light. There was something foreign about these twelve faces—something of the primitive Tartar, which has long been effaced among the peoples of the Mongolian frontier regions. While the other Mongols let the peaceful, restful atmosphere of the time and the place take possession of them, these twelve sat as though on springs, ready to fly or to leap to arms.

What were these twelve rough children of the desert doing in this sanctuary, whose gods inspired exalted, abstract contemplation ? What were the offerings which Lamadjab had laid before the golden pagoda ? And what princess was it who had given her name to this remote idyllic temple ? I glanced at Lamadjab and old Puntsuk. The first was a typical Eastern Mongolian aristocrat, whose features showed signs of Manchurian racial kinship. Puntsuk was a picture of fatherly mildness.

I put a searching question to Puntsuk. His eyes wandered towards the fire, through barriers of time and place, and when he began to speak, it was like listening to an echo from a time long past. We went back to the pass where Khabto Khasar had stood centuries ago, and where we had camped the night before, and we followed the descendants of the father of the race into a new century of their saga. . . .

Bodachi was Khabto Khasar's descendant in the fourteenth generation, and emissaries from the chief of the Manchus came to him asking for help. The Chinese Ming dynasty, which had overthrown the Mongolian power in China, was now to be driven out and a descendant of the nomads restored to the Dragon Throne in Peking. So Bodachi sent express messengers through the camps with orders to all men fit to bear arms, and the scions of Khabto Khasar's " knife-sharp " warriors, tired of peace, once more broke away from their quiet mountain idyll to taste the sweets of victory and unbridled savagery. Once more hordes under the standards adorned with yaks' tails galloped over China's rice-fields, and all resistance was trampled down under their horse-hooves. When the last resistance was broken, and homesickness called Bodachi and his warriors back to the grass tracks from which they could see the peaceful snows of the Bayan Jeruke mountain, the chief of the Manchus had become the ruler of China and sat on the Dragon Throne in Peking as founder of the Manchu dynasty.

From that day onwards the chiefs of the Jasaktu country rode to Peking every year to exchange pledges of friendship with the Son of Heaven. Khabto Khasar's seventeenth descendant in the chief's tent of the Jasaktu Mongols was called Todbadjamso. And when Todbadjamso's son, Saadgum, had reached years of discretion, he accompanied his father over the " road with the forty-seven passes " to see the Son of Heaven in the Forbidden City of Peking.

One evening, when young Prince Saadgum was walking by the lotus ponds that surround the Forbidden City of Peking, he saw a sight which fascinated him. Leaning against the railing of one of the crescent-shaped marble bridges, which crossed the canal round the Forbidden City, stood a young woman. The setting sun brought to life the colours and patterns on her flowing silk robe and lent a transfigured beauty

to her eggshell-pale face. In the picture which she so completely dominated were fat eunuchs, waving long peacock's-feather fans, and slave-girls eager to anticipate her wishes. The young nomad had never seen or dreamed of such beauty; it intoxicated him, and in steppe fashion he ran forward to grasp his prize. But before he reached the object of his desire, a wall of swords and halberds sprang up between him and her, and he was a helpless spectator as she was swiftly led away. Once, before eunuchs and slaves had hidden her behind the dense foliage of the acacias, she had turned to look at the disturber of her contemplation—the fiery youth with weather-beaten face, strong teeth and fierce eyes—and the prince had seen one flashing glance which he interpreted as a promise. From that hour Prince Saadgum was transformed. He forsook all the attractions of Peking and his friends' wild carouses. Every evening at sunset he went to the marble bridge leading to the Forbidden City to see the vision again, but the palace eunuchs, armed and incorruptible, always stood at the top of the bridge. The crickets chirped in mockery among the lotuses of the pond, and the princess never returned.

Then the visit ended, and the Mongols went back to the desert. But not even the winds of the steppe could sweep the grief out of Saadgum's heart, for when he left Peking he knew that the maiden to whom he had given his love was Princess Erh Fu, the favourite daughter of the Emperor himself, and to him inaccessible.

The excitement of hunting no longer attracted him, and he let his hawks fly away over the mountains. The fire in his tent burned quiet and warm, and he made his singer sing the words that came into his (Saadgum's) mind. The songs that resulted were love-songs.

One day the singer went to Todbadjamso and sang to him all the songs which reflected young Prince Saadgum's sorrowing heart, and the father understood. Next time he rode to Peking to exchange pledges of friendship with the Son of Heaven, the young prince lay dying in his tent, and Todbadjamso took with him his youngest and most loved daughter.

When he stood at the foot of the Dragon Throne, he held his daughter by the hand and offered her as tribute; he heaped all the treasures of the wild before the Emperor and reminded him of the doughty men of his people who had helped to set the Manchu dynasty on the throne of China.

That year the Emperor of China and the chieftain of the

THE PRINCESS'S TEMPLE

Jasaktu Mongols concluded a pact of friendship and exchanged their favourite daughters.

So the young Manchu princess had to quit the refined world of Peking and set on the long cold journey over the "forty-seven passes" into the distant unknown, where a nomad's tent was to be her home and herds of cattle her riches. She sat like a delicate, rare flower behind the wind-tattered curtains of the palanquin, while the bearers toiled forward through the endless, storm-swept wilderness.

She was moving farther and farther away from the world of her childhood; her imperial father sat alone in the Forbidden City, more and more preoccupied with her future. And to make things easier for her and to quiet his own conscience, he sent seven chosen men after her. These were seven artists from the North Manchurian forests—masters in turning the raw wealth of Nature to refined beauty, in building palaces and temples from the trunks of the forest, and in making ornaments worthy of an Emperor's daughter from the silver and precious stones of the mountains.

Thus the Manchu princess Erh Fu came to the wild country of the Jasaktu Mongols as the symbol of all that was beautiful and delicate; she became a mystic revelation to those of her time and an unforgettable memory to posterity.

Her imperial father did not need to weep for her, for the fierce flame that had sprung up in the prince's heart at their first meeting had been reflected in her own. And when the seven Manchurian craftsmen came to the Jasaktu country, the prince set them to build temples and palaces, while the princess accompanied him on his rough hunting expeditions and sat by his tent fire—for they loved one another. . . .

Puntsuk checked his rapid story and made a sign which sent one of the twelve hunters after fresh tea. This was offered first to Lamadjab, and the serving-man now seemed to treat him with even greater deference than before. Puntsuk knocked his long pipe out into the chafing-dish and made no sign to have it refilled. And the whole circle of men seemed to feel that the evening's story had now reached a happy ending.

I also felt this, but—the presence of the twelve hunters in this Buddhist sanctuary, the golden pagoda behind the altar, and the leading part which Lamadjab and the twelve hunters had played in that unorthodox sacrificial ceremony? I wanted to have it all explained before I could find rest in my sleeping bag.

I offered Puntsuk my box of Capstan, and to my relief he filled his long pipe again.

"And the prince and princess," I asked, when I saw his first puff of smoke, "did they live long and happily? And when the princess died, was she taken back to her own country, as Chinese traditions require?"

Puntsuk smiled at my impatient curiosity. Then he continued gently, as though he understood that my question was dictated by more than curiosity: "The prince and princess did live long, and their happiness ended at the same time, for the proximity of the one was the happiness of the other. Before the princess died, she had set her Manchus to build this temple and appointed it to be her last resting-place, and the prince had her mortal remains built into the golden pagoda behind the altar of the main temple. When that happened, the prince had become chief of the tribe, and he gave the three of the princess's seven Manchus who were still alive riches and free grazing up in the northern mountains."

I studied the un-Mongolian traces which were visible in Lamadjab's face, and glanced at the twelve hunters' sloping foreheads and high cheek-bones. They reminded me of Tunguses, and the home of the Tunguses lay up in the forests of Northern Manchuria.

Puntsuk's last words were an echo of my thoughts. " The three Manchus received both land and riches," he said, " but in return they had to bind themselves to make twelve of their sons keep guard eternally at their mistress's tomb, and every year on this day the twelve were to support the prince and his descendants at the annual sacrifice. Since then fourteen generations have passed away ; the descendants of the prince and the three Manchus have lived through them, and our race has not yet forgotten its traditions. Lamadjab is the descendant of Prince Saadgum and Princess Erh Fu in the fourteenth generation, Khabto Khasar's descendant in the thirty-second generation, and the Jasaktu Mongols' only rightful lord."

It had grown late. Two of the hunters spread Lamadjab's couch for the night, and the twelve men, after bending the knee to their young master, left us.

Puntsuk knocked his pipe out again, and I offered him no more tobacco. I followed the twelve men out into the temple court. The stars were as brilliant as they only can be among high mountains. Around us the mountain crests shone in the starlight like a protecting wall of unapproachable purity, and an unnoticed puff of wind made the little bells on the temple roof strike up a complete symphony of silvery notes. I was indescribably happy to feel that there was still such a spot upon earth.

The twelve hunters were just turning in, but I had still one unanswered question which threatened to disturb my night's rest. I asked an old greybeard: "How many children have you twelve altogether, and where are they?"

He ran his eyes over his comrades while he counted on his fingers. "Three," he replied, rather ashamed, "but we should have been more if all the children born had lived."

"Three!" I repeated, slightly disappointed; "then you will be the last full guard at Khatun Sume."

"Oh, no," he answered with a cheerful grin. "Avo, our father up in Manchu Ail, has more than seven hundred children, so we are stronger than ever."

A multitude of questions formed themselves in my mind, but I asked no more. "Our father in Manchu Ail with the seven hundred children?" It sounded like a romance one could not fathom by asking questions. It was something one had to find out for oneself.

IN CAMP AT MANCHU AIL

ON a radiant October day Sangerup and I started from the rail-head in the Khorchin country and took a road which soon divided into many rough tracks.

Our travelling companions were four young Mongols who had never before visited the wild country to the north. To them the northern mountains signified something remote and alien, which must be approached with great caution, and all they knew of our destination, Manchu Ail, was that it was the resort of dangerous characters.

Our route lay through the Solon mountains, whose name indicates that the Solon horde, in old times a powerful warrior race, but now broken up into small disconnected fragments in the remotest corners of Central Asia, once had its headquarters in this wild region.

From Solon we followed the " river of wealth " in among the lower spurs of the mountains, till we came to the " Muses'

Stream ", whose porcelain-blue water babbled between lush green banks along the narrow valley. Slowly we climbed through silent uninhabited spaces towards the high sources of the stream, and halted at " Three Lanterns Pass ".

It was clear that we were on the borders of a vigilant wilderness community. Primitive fortifications made of boulders flung together could be seen on all the dominating heights of the pass, and in the middle of its saddle-back rose a high natural altar, hung with Lamaistic praying flags and bones inscribed with the magic formulæ of a primitive religion.

On the other side of the pass, fifty yards down, lay a white tent, from which a party of rough fellows came to meet us. They barely replied to our greetings and did not bid us welcome, but questioned us closely about the destination and object of our journey, while their searching eyes ran over our persons and baggage.

" The road to Manchu Ail is barred," they cried menacingly. We should act wisely, they added, if we guided our horses straight back towards the southern lowlands.

They were a rough, hostile crowd. Their hard faces were furrowed by wind and weather, and their black looks showed that none of them set much value on a man's life, either his own or his neighbour's. Suddenly their leader advanced towards us with so violent a movement that our horses reared.

" Look at me ! " he yelled in a voice which awoke all the echoes of the mountain, " and if you know me again, betray me to the Chinese mandarin down there ! I have found shelter and protection from the chief at Manchu Ail, and I shall flee no farther."

His men had crowded round him again, and some of them were fingering their long knives. Their fanatical eyes flickered nervously, and there was a threatening tone in their mumbling voices.

Only old Sangerup remained perfectly calm. He advanced slowly towards the group of men, gazing at their leader with a

curiosity which in the circumstances seemed impudent. Suddenly he shouted, as loud as his old voice could :
" Græda Merin, don't you know me ? I'm Sangerup ! "
These words seemed to have a magic effect. All those stern men were transformed into laughing children ; tears of joy at the reunion streamed down their leathery, weather-beaten cheeks.

No one gave any further thought to me or my young Mongols. Slowly, full of wonder, we followed the old men, who, grinning and gesticulating, were hurrying towards the white tent, the first tent in the Manchu Ail country. We spent the evening crowded together in Græda Merin's tent, and we were all as happy as reunited brothers.

While Sangerup described the political revolution which had taken place in their homeland since they last had news from the outside world, I contemplated the circle of old faces, illuminated by the flickering light of the fire. Their nervous watchfulness gradually diminished ; their eyes became gentle and at last came to rest in the warm glow of the fire. When the time was ripe, they began, as old men do, to tell of the days when they were all young and happy in a happy country. The many stories they told centred round Græda Merin's name and, strung together, formed the story of his life and his life's struggle.

Late in the evening Sangerup summed up the evening's talk in a song ; the tune was old, but its words were inspired by the great joy of the reunion.

There was a time, when old age was far off,
when there was a chief, to whom the young could give their strength,
when Græda Merin was the first among thousands of warriors—
and we thought our youth would be eternal in a happy land.

One day trouble came to the steppe, and Græda Merin and his warriors
followed the chieftain to protect the peace of the steppes.
But the Khorchin people's steel bit no longer, and the attackers'
new weapons mowed down the tribe's best warriors,
and all the riches and strength of the tribe vanished.

And when the country was deprived of its strength
the mandarin would deprive the people of their freedom also,
and when Græda Merin tried to assemble the tribe's last strength
for resistance,
he was imprisoned and tortured.

And when his wife, who stood outside the prison,
heard his screams, she went up into the mountains
and came back with ten men of her race,
who freed her lord.

After the deed Græda Merin's wife and her following
were declared outlaws,
and to share her fate,
Græda Merin killed the mandarin
who had outlawed his wife
and made him homeless.

From that day on Græda Merin vowed his life to the fight against
the oppressors,
and many Khorchin Mongols fell under his banner.

In 1921 the Chinese sent an army to the Khorchin country to stamp out Græda Merin and his fighters for freedom. There was a last battle in the Solon mountains. Græda Merin and seven of his warriors were the only survivors, and his wife was among the killed.

The mandarin put a large reward on their heads, and they were chased about among the mountains for a long time, but at last they found a refuge with the old chief of Manchu Ail, where the Chinese did not dare come and look for them. The eight men had lived since then at Manchu Ail, and till the day of our meeting they did not know that the Chinese had been driven out of their country again and that the Japanese had come into power there. When I awoke next morning, Sangerup and Græda Merin had ridden to the main camp of Manchu Ail, and when they returned at midday they were able to tell me that I was welcome to the chief's guest tent.

IN CAMP AT MANCHU AIL

It was evening when we approached the valley in the middle of which the chief's camp lay. Dark mountain walls surrounded the valley, and the sharp peaks shone out ghostlike against a sky which trembled with stars. The whole landscape seemed petrified, remote from the world, unreal.

I had often noticed that the word Avo, which means father, very often occurred in the Mongols' conversation when the chief of this mountain region was spoken of, and now, while we were on our way to his camp, Sangerup gave me the explanation of this.

The people in Manchu Ail were all descendants of the Manchurian craftsmen who had accompanied Princess Erh Fu from Peking to the Khorchin country. In the course of time the men at Manchu Ail had married Mongol girls, and the members of the community, which now numbered about seven hundred, were called Manchu Mongols. The chief, who was always the head of this numerous tribe, was called by everyone Avo (father), and this name had with the passage of time become synonymous with the title of chief.

Suddenly the cries of herdsmen rang out, and a ghostlike procession of dark silhouettes of cattle emerged from a cleft in the mountains. Then the flickering columns of smoke from the tent camps became visible, and a pack of baying watch-dogs rushed to meet us. We rode into a group of a dozen tents through an opening in a stockade, and when the women of the camp had caught the furious dogs, we dismounted.

The blanket before the entrance to the main tent was drawn aside, and we crept in and took the guests' places by the fire,

the leading hearth of Manchu Ail. Right in front of us, on a couch of hides and wolves' skins, lay the chief; he was so old that the four elders who sat by his side looked like vigorous men. Two of them were playing chess, while the three others were entirely absorbed in the course of the game. After a hurried glance in our direction, they bent over the chess-board again and recommenced their preoccupied mumblings.

Harness, bows and full quivers were hung about the sides of the tent, and in one corner stood the most delightful collection of old musical instruments. A thick camel's-hair rope hung between two tent posts, and to it were attached a number of tufts of hair and wool from slaughtered beasts, while from a row of wild pigs' teeth, fastened to the tent wall, dangled bladders and sheepskins sewn together, full of kumiss and other delicacies. Not so much as an aluminium cup or an enamel dish had found its way to this camp, and the tent smelt of past ages.

After the game was over, Græda Merin approached the oldest of the five elders to exchange all the polite old-time greetings, after which the five were able to show a friendly interest in us without risking their dignity. Now they no longer attempted to conceal their great curiosity ; question and answer followed each other quickly across the fire, till the atmosphere became quite confidential.

Then the women came with a great copper dish on which lay a sheep roasted whole. The animal's unskinned legs and glistening fat tail hung over the edge of the dish, and on top of the steaming meat lay the sheep's cooked head.

The men had all turned their sleeves up above the elbows and unsheathed their long knives, and they now sat and followed the chief's movements with greedy eyes. With a few quick strokes he cut a cross on the sheep's forehead, after which he carved a few lumps of meat; these he laid upon the tent altar and the flames of the fire. The rest of the meat was cut up and placed on large wooden dishes, which were laid before us. Eating now began with incredible vigour. . .

Gongerer, a grinning servant, covered with dirt and full of enjoyment, poured kumiss from the filled goat-skins into our silver-mounted cups. The tent was soon thick with the heat engendered by digestion, and the sweat ran from the greasy wine-inflamed faces. Outside the tent dogs stood at every chink, sniffing with satisfaction, and now and then we caught a glimpse of an active boy nipping in to secure a half-gnawed bone.

The chief was a good host, and at last we all became so heavy with food and dulled with drink that we sank into comfortable attitudes.

A few women came in carrying new-born calves and lambs ; these were thrown down in one corner of the hot tent to escape the night's cold, and the feeble lowing and bleating of the new-born beasts mingled with the Mongols' satisfied eructations. Some of the Mongols stripped their perspiring bodies to the waist, and two of the old men were scratching the chief's shining sweaty back.

An atmosphere of indescribable well-being and peace spread through the tent, and the old musical instruments began to pass from hand to hand among the men; the young men sang of Djangsara Anga, the girl of many qualities, while the old, who were long past thoughts of love, extolled the deeds of their fathers and of their own youth.

The tent fire burned slowly down to a deep glow, and as the fire sank the tent became quieter. A few of the old men had fallen asleep, and the bright night stars became visible through the smoke-vent.

I stayed a month at Manchu Ail, and when I left the place—a survival from an age gone by—I took with me a rich collection of tunes, legends, ethnographic details, and much else that formed the milieu of those primitive people, who had lived the life of a past age right into our noisy modern times. Once more I had been vouchsafed the great joy which comes to a research worker when, instead of reading and dreaming himself into the time that interests him, he actually experiences it.

One always longs to have over again a time such as that which I spent in the camps up in the Solon mountains; but I shall never see the Manchu Ail camps again. Since my stay there the Japanese storm-flood has swept over Asia, and it has destroyed the isolation which the Chinese never dared to threaten. The little community in Manchu Ail, whose families had grazed their cattle there for centuries, is now scattered to the winds.

Women and old men have been evacuated to places of smaller strategic importance, and the men fit to bear arms are riding as assault troops in the great Japanese advance. The young men of Manchu Ail, once so overflowing with life and spirits, are now learning discipline and much else that is new from Japanese teachers down in the new lowland cities.

When, a year later, I passed by one of the new schools in the lowlands, I met Gongerer, the lad who had been our cup-bearer at the feast in Manchu Ail, and who then had been so dirty, cheerful and boisterous. Now he was clean, but his irresistible savage grin was diminished to a controlled smile. All his dreams of becoming a horse-breaker and one of the great hunters of the desert were forgotten. He had now quite other objects in view, which I could not understand because he could not explain them to me—and perhaps because they were quite foreign to us both.

AMONG DEVIL DANCERS IN THE KING'S MONASTERY

IMMEDIATELY before I started on my journey home after my first Mongolian expedition, I stayed in Peking for a week.

I spent most of this time with an elderly Manchurian princess who had spent her childhood and earliest youth in the mysterious atmosphere of the Forbidden City.

After the fall of the Manchu dynasty in 1912 she was a feted guest at international diplomatic dinners in Peking, where she charmed everyone with her exotic beauty, her acute intelligence, and the atmosphere of mystery which she brought with her from the Forbidden City. But years had passed, and she was now forgotten amid the ceaseless unrest and political tension that had effaced the old-world idyll whose worshipped incarnation she had once been.

She had retired to one of the old pavilions which lean against the massive walls of the imperial city, to seek refuge in memories of the time when she was the old Empress Dowager's youngest and last maid of honour—before she had been " discovered ", deified and at last forgotten by her capricious foreign friends. I had been told that she now spent her time in examining the almost inaccessible documents of the Forbidden City, and I had sought her out in the hope of getting an historical check on some of the fantastic legends I had lately heard in the Manchurian desert which was the original home of her race.

I found Princess Shou Shan Yü in a hall whose dilapidation only enhanced its beauty. Everywhere, in niches and on shelves, stood porcelain, the shape and colour of which harmonized beautifully with the old coloured wood of the carved wall panels.

" You call it K'ang Hsi," the Princess said to me, smiling, with a graceful gesture towards the ceramic feast of colour. " To you, K'ang Hsi means just the porcelain works of art your museums want, and with you the name K'ang Hsi will survive only so long as there are still people who treat beautiful brittle things with care and reverence. But to me K'ang Hsi means much more than that. He was my great ancestor, the third of our clan who sat on the Dragon Throne, and the one who brought the greatest glory to our dynasty."

Then she made me a present of her store of knowledge, and I learned things which I had never read or heard of.

What particularly interested me was the information that the great K'ang Hsi was three parts Mongol by birth. He had grown up in the world of imagination of his Mongolian mother, and for twenty-seven of his most vigorous years as a ruler—the years in which he abandoned the imperial city and its luxury to build up his mighty empire by long and toilsome journeys—he had had his Mongolian grandmother on his father's side to steady and support him. These two nomad women, his mother and grandmother, were both chiefs' daughters of the Mongolian Khorchin tribe.

Khorchin—Mongolian Khorchin—which to Princess Shou Shan Yü was only a name from old palace annals, something vague and distant, belonging to the past and the unknown desert world, was the country which I had just passed through and to whose people I had listened. And I told her the legends which throw light on the early days of the Khorchin tribe and which still live in the nomads' camps.

No one less than Khabto Khasar himself, the great Jenghiz Khan's famous brother, had led the Khorchin people from Siberia's snows to Manchuria's alluring fertility. And when Jenghiz Khan, at the beginning of the thirteenth century, led

his Mongols on the great campaign against China, Khabto Khasar and his warriors had protected the left flank of the horde so vigorously that Jenghiz Khan had given them the title of honour Khorchin, the " knife-sharp ".

Four centuries later, when the Manchus, who had become the Khorchin people's neighbours to the east, became active, Khorchin was ruled by Bodachi, who was Khabto Khasar's descendant in the fourteenth generation. Bodachi united his " knife-sharp " cavalry with the Manchurian bowmen, and the two peoples fought side by side at the taking of Peking. In 1644 the chief of the Manchus was placed on the Dragon Throne.

The first great Manchu emperors, who still possessed the instincts of the desert, in deep gratitude, often and richly rewarded their Mongolian brothers-in-arms.

Once, when a Khorchin chief's wild son had been tamed and softened by his love for the favourite daughter of a Manchu emperor, the emperor had sent the girl to the remote nomad tents of the chief's son. The emperor's gently nurtured daughter had borne her lord sons, and from that day there was Manchu blood in Khabto Khasar's line of chiefs in the Khorchin country.

AMONG DEVIL DANCERS IN THE KING'S MONASTERY

Twilight had fallen in the little Peking pavilion ; a servant came in carrying lights and a large bronze chafing-dish, which he placed between us. And with the new light and its countless reflections the atmosphere of the room changed.

The princess sat bowed over the chafing-dish ; its embers threw soft colours on the silken folds of her dress. Her black eyes were bright with eagerness, and her questions came slowly and dreamily as though across a nomad's camp fire. She asked about the steppe and its nature, the Khorchin people and its life. I answered her questions and told her of Lamadjab, Khabto Khasar's descendant in the Khorchin country, whose ancestress was one of her own line.

Our conversations arose from old palace documents and legends from the Khorchin people's camp fires. They gave rise to many questions and answers, leading up to the last time I saw Lamadjab—the time we saw the " Devil Dance " together in the remote " King's Monastery ".

From Manchu Ail I continued my journey in old Sangerup's company to the " King's Monastery ", for we had heard that the time for the annual great ceremony of the monastery was near.

After an eleven-days' journey we reached " Mountain Goat Pass ". Before us lay a smiling plateau, of a shape which the Mongols describe with the word " table ". A river, whose course we had followed, and which so far had raged foaming over the falls and obstacles of the narrow mountain clefts, was here transformed into a broad blue ribbon, flowing noiselessly between lush grass banks.

Later the river turned into a wide valley and passed through a small lake, in whose pure crystal-clear water the green leaves of a poplar grove were reflected. The valley was framed by low red-brown hills, and in the north rose a pyramid-shaped mountain, from whose slopes white walls glittered in the sun. A dreamlike silence lay over the whole landscape. It was the kind of valley which the hardy nomads fill in their imagination with herds of cattle and horses and many white tents—such a landscape as provides the frame for many Mongolian adventures.

We sat down to enjoy the place and the atmosphere, and Sangerup had to take out his pipe to express his feelings. He recounted the legends of the river and the history of the monastery.

On a hunting expedition along this river, the great Khabto Khasar sent one of his unfailing arrows at a stag. He had struck it so surely that its life-blood spurted from its heart, so that it had only fifty paces to run. But with its last leap the doomed beast flung itself into the river, and when the water washed over it its wounds were healed, and it disappeared unharmed on the other side of the river. The hunters had followed its tracks to a grotto in the hillside ; but when they entered the grotto to kill their booty, they found, not a stag, but a holy hermit. This was Namserai, the earthly reincarnation of joy ; he had called them to him, and had promised Khabto Khasar to stand by him and his tribe for ever, if they called upon him every year on that day and in that place.

Khabto Khasar had erected his most sacred temple tent before the entrance to the grotto. He had filled it with his most famous wizards and holy men, and had enjoined upon posterity never to abandon the rites which perpetuated the magic power of the place. The Khorchin chiefs of Khabto Khasar's line had obeyed their ancestor's command, and the Khorchin people had remained happy until our presumptuous modern times.

Once when the Emperor K'ang Hsi was bowed down and heavy with grief and melancholy, the Khorchin chief of the day took him to the holy place, and the emperor had there regained happiness. To show his reverence for God and his gratitude to the chief, K'ang Hsi caused a splendid monastery to be erected on the spot ; it came to be called " the King's Monastery ".

When Sangerup had finished his story, he sat in silence for a long time. Then he pointed to the white remnants of wall on the mountain slope opposite. " Over there is what still remains of the Emperor K'ang Hsi's monastery."

We followed the river through the sacrificial grove, which was full of old stone altars, and approached the white fragments of wall. At the entrance to the cloister we were received by three old priests, and we sat down together to exchange friendly words.

And while the sun was sinking, I sat and listened to fateful reminiscences. I was carried back twenty-one years in time to *Khara Holerens Djil*, " Black Mouse's Year ". The Chinese robber generals, who then held sway in the Manchurian frontier districts, looked long at fertile Khorchin and decided to fill their bottomless war chest from the rich nomad country.

AMONG DEVIL DANCERS IN THE KING'S MONASTERY

General Wu was sent out on to the steppes to rob the Mongols of their wealth.

The Khorchin chief had called up all his warriors to offer resistance. But when "Black Mouse's Year" was over, the

flower of the Khorchin country's manhood had been mown down, temples and monasteries levelled to the earth, herds of horses and cattle carried off—and the generation which was now twenty summers old had unknown Chinese fathers.

"Before the Chinese looting one could sit up here in the King's Monastery and count horses and cattle in tens of thousands," was Sangerup's melancholy recollection. "And to-day all that remains of the temple's riches is twenty sheep," the priest replied. "Namserai has forgotten us."

The last gleam of sun was effaced, and darkness sank over the valley. And with the dark came the measured drone of the temple drums and the mumble of the priests conducting service from the interior of the monastery. The three old priests rose, and we followed them in among the ruins of the monastery. Through the remains of gateways and roofless halls we approached that part of it which had been restored by unskilful hands. And with the three priests as guides we entered the gloomy obscurity of the temple, amid the noise of unseen drums and mumbling voices. We felt our way carefully forward towards the interior of the temple—pillars and unseen objects blocked the way everywhere. A faint oil light was lit, and one of the priests led us to a low couch of boards.

Only when our eyes had grown accustomed to the semi-darkness did we perceive the *gurtum* of the temple, wearing his fantastic ceremonial garb. He was so old that it was impossible to tell his age. He wore on his head a hat gleaming with metal, with a crown of long knives, and along the brim of the hat hung silver ornaments fabricated in the form of skulls. He held in his hands a spear, adorned with a yak's tail, and rattling chains.

This was the night of the year when the return of Namserai to this place can be expected, the night of the year when he is reincarnated in the *gurtum's* body to point out the way to happiness.

In the shadow, at the *gurtum's* feet, a young man sat, his face turned towards the old man. There was something in his strong, supple form which marked him out from the age and decay of his surroundings.

The measured beat of the temple drums grew louder, and seven little oil lamps flared up in the background. In this new light all the mysteries of the temple, till then only guessed, became visible to us. Fantastic devil masks grinned from the smoke-blackened back wall, while stags' and yaks' heads butted at the flickering shadows of the hall. Along the walls appeared the yellow-robed forms of lamas, drumming and intoning, and long temple horns pointed towards the open centre of the hall. Dented images gleamed behind the oil lamps, and meat and other offerings lay heaped on the altar table at their feet.

Then the three old priests came in wearing full-length

brocade robes. They took down from the back wall the grotesque animal masks which were their symbols, and formed up round the *gurtum* transformed into sinister devils. And while the drone of the drums rose and mingled with the long horn instruments' discordant fanfares, the three men began the ceremonial devil dance—they were the three last of a once large circle of devils. They waved and gesticulated with their lean arms; their weary legs pirouetted furiously as they strove to follow the noisy music.

Suddenly a shiver of ecstasy went through the *gurtum*. He rose swaying from his high seat, and, shaking and muttering, tottered towards the door of the temple. The intoning of the priests and the beating of the drums accompanied him. . . .

" Namserai is coming," Sangerup cried at my side. The young man at the *gurtum's* feet had jumped up to accompany and support the old man. Again and again he shouted the same question in the *gurtum's* face : " Where shall I find the way to happiness, the strength of my line and the freedom of my tribe ? "

The *gurtum* started violently at the young man's cry. Drops of sweat fell from his ravaged face and inarticulate gibberish from his foaming lips : his bloodshot eyes wavered between the young man's determined gaze and his own remote visions. Swooning, he turned towards the circle of intoning and drumming priests as if imploring their help, and the music rose to a wild crescendo. He stood for a moment as though straining to hear and see into the remote future ; but that was the end, and the old *gurtum* collapsed and slid slowly to the ground between the young man's arms. Namserai had left him again—without having imparted to him any of his great knowledge.

The devil dance was over, and with it the *gurtum's* search for the way to happiness. The noise of the horns subsided ; only monotonous drum-beats were still heard, and the temple lamps were flickering out.

The young man stood for a moment contemplating the helplessness around him—the old man groaning at his feet, the three old priests with their grotesque masks, the vandalized images and the tattered temple banners. Then he shook himself defiantly, and as he passed close to me I saw and recognized his face. It was Lamadjab, Khabto Khasar's last descendant, the desert-born son of the overthrown Manchu dynasty.

Next morning Sangerup and I continued our journey to a new destination, but before we started I visited the chief actors in the night's drama. The *gurtum* lay in a deathlike trance, the three old priests looked more depressed than ever, and

Lamadjab had cast off his old-time dress. "The past is past," he said in a voice more resolute than the look in his eyes. "Now we must seek new roads to find a future." When I started he gave me his best wishes for my journey.

When I had related my reminiscences of the wilderness to Princess Shou Shan Yü, I could not resist the temptation to let her hear the message which Lamadjab had given me for my journey, and which contained many good wishes from the

nomads to their friend. In his message he repeated the word *Jabonah*, the word which through the ages has been the master-word of the nomad language, one which will ring out over Asia's deserts and steppes so long as their people are free to follow their instincts—it is the word which means setting off to continue a journey.

I saw that Lamadjab's message kindled new life in her delicate features, as though it had touched a string within her that had been long unused, but still could sound. "He speaks good words, my young kinsman. You must bring us together some day," she said to me as a kind of answer to his message.

They will both live in my memory as two of the dearest

people I have known—these latter-day representatives of two of Asia's oldest and once mightiest families. But it will never be granted to me to bring them together, for Prince Lamadjab fell two months later in the battle of Dolo Nor.

STEPPE POETRY

SANGERUP was my companion and confidant on several of my journeys. My reason for choosing him was that he was said to have a great knowledge of the old songs. In his youth he had sung old-time poetry, rich in meaning, to the great men of the steppe, and drinking songs at his comrades' festive gatherings; but now he had survived them all, and the new generation wanted to hear quite different songs from those he had treasured up.

Sangerup was over seventy, and the vigour of life had left him; but now my interest in all the memories he had so long brooded over alone seemed to make him younger every day.

Sangerup means "he who can do everything", and his knowledge was manifold. He knew the birds' songs, he could interpret the rustling of the wind in the steppe grass; the depths of the mountains and the life of the stars had no secrets from him. He was in intimate contact with all nature, and he became my guide to all the camps where the olden time still survived.

We were travelling across the Barga steppe towards Naidung Djalan's camp when we met Bantje. Our meeting-place was in the neighbourhood of a little salt lake, surrounded by a grey powdery salt steppe, monotonous and lifeless. Bantje was blind, and wherever he went he saw only the beauty of his distant homeland.

He had been blind for thirty years, and for all that time he had been wandering among the camps which are inhabited by Mongols. When he lost his sight and could no longer be of use in his home camp, he abandoned its hearth to spread the gift of song by alien camp fires.

He had grown old; the camps had decreased in number; and it was seldom that he was received with pleasure.

Once many years ago I had met him right up in Northern Mongolia. Then he was dressed in silk and rode a fine horse. Now he looked poor and miserable, and his only companion was a fatherless lad. They both went on foot; the lad found the way through the desert, and the old man followed him, guided by the stick of which each held an end.

Bantje's companion was the sole survivor of a once rich and populous camp in the Keshikt country. When he was still a child, the camp was devastated by a robber band, which killed all its inhabitants and plundered its wealth.

Luckily the child was asleep while the robbers were devastating the camp, and so had escaped his friends' fate; and luckily he had screamed with terror when Bantje, later, was passing the place. The blind man had taken the child with him, and as all who knew his name were now dead, Bantje had christened him Surong. Since then fifteen years had passed, and during this time the two had never been separated.

That evening I spent in camp with wise old Sangerup, blind Bantje and homeless Surong. While the rest of us were busy with animals and tents, Bantje sat by the fire and moved his fingers through the grass and over everything which lay within his reach. Now and then he bent forward towards the fire, as if trying to interpret the crackling of the flames. Then he raised his weather-beaten face to the pale light of the stars, and got the feel of his surroundings with all the sensitiveness of the blind. He called his young foster-son to him, and it was clear that they were talking of the scenery which framed the night's dreaming-place.

Surong described with soft words the blue horizon of the mountains that lay about us, and when the old man had become completely familiar with his surroundings, he called for his instrument. For a while he sat tuning its strings by the warm fire, and collecting his thoughts. Then he sang:

A strange child was abandoned and alone.
The mist spread over the steppe like a sea—I came nearer.
The red of the sinking sun was vast as a mountain. . . .
In the dark one needs a friend's hand.

When one meets a friend, when one meets a little child,
one's heart is soft as melted lead.
However high the mountain, one must ascend it.
However deep the forest, one can always clear a path through it. . .
Of life and death only the gods know.

We had all found places by the blaze; the immense vault of night rose around us. Sangerup had taken out his pipe, and having sat for a while watching the smoke mount and disappear through the vent, he sang to the others' accompaniment:

> If one rides a good horse, the way is never long.
> It is on a long journey that a friend's value is tried.
> If you would know the fineness of gold,
> rub it till it becomes worn.

When we continued our journey, Bantje and Surong had found places on our least heavily loaded pack-horses. After two days' marches we left the barren steppe and entered one of the valleys which lead into the heart of the Hsingan mountains.

It was early autumn, and a night's frost had splashed the wooded mountain slopes with fire without effacing the soft colours of the abundant meadow flowers in the valley. Down the middle of the valley the river babbled blue and clear like an eager message from the glittering snow-peaks in the background. Bantje's young guide often stopped him, and both dismounted so that the old man might inhale the scent of the wild flowers and feel the lush vegetation with his fingers. Graceful deer crossed our path in flight, and the rays of the autumn sun gleamed in the gay plumage of fluttering pheasants.

Surong bounded up and down in his saddle in sheer enthusiasm, and the lad's delight brought a song to Bantje's lips :

When the stag runs, it strikes the sky with its hind hooves.
The pheasant has all its feathers strewn with gold
when it flies through the sunshine.
The little hare too is pretty, reflected in the river's shining water.

For three days we followed the valley as it climbed slowly. The clear stream became white as chalk with foaming glacier water ; we passed the tracks of bears, and on dominating hilltops the twisted horns of ibexes were printed against the clear autumn sky.

Towards evening we overtook two bear-hunters; my travelling companions were delighted to meet them again, and the hunters likewise.

"Aha!" they cried. "Now we shall have another evening's sing-song! And we've got food, we shall enjoy that too!" They pointed grinning to their horses, labouring under the weight of the killed bears.

These were Naidung Djalan's two sons, returning from a successful hunting expedition. They were full of curiosity about everything that had happened down on the steppes, but they did not want immediate and exhaustive answers to their questions—they only wanted to be sure that the newcomers possessed the knowledge they desired. They did not want to hear and discuss the news in all its detail till we had reached the fire of the home camp, and a festive meal had provided the right atmosphere.

We rode over the pass, and below, on the other side, lay Naidung Djalan's autumn camp. Its eight tents lay like a pale bunch of flowers against a green mountain meadow, so large and fertile that there was grazing for huge herds of cattle. But Naidung Djalan had not moved to this out-of-the-way place until the robbers in his home district had stripped him of all his wealth in cattle, and he and his sons had only become bear-hunters in this remote region to preserve their freedom to the last.

The barking camp dogs rushed towards us, and women and children swarmed out of the tents to catch them. The members of the little hunting community were delighted to see Bantje and Sangerup. The women came with their long knives to start cutting up and cooking the bears, and the children flung themselves upon the animals' bloody skins.

The elders of the camp led us to the guest tent, where we exchanged dignified greetings with old Naidung Djalan. As soon as we had taken the places of honour on the western side of the altar table, the other members of the camp began to assemble. They were all dressed in soft deerskins, and carried long two-edged knives.

Naidung Djalan's face had been disfigured by a bear's paw, but the many furs which covered the floor and sides of the tent showed that he had taken an ample revenge. From the altar a gentle-faced image of Buddha gazed out at the many guns, spears and other hunting implements which hung on the walls.

Naidung Djalan's wife came in and blew life into the fire, and soon quantities of bear's meat were being cooked in the great guests' pot.

Now and then politenesses were exchanged over the fire, but the strong smell of food confused our thoughts and checked all conversation. Naidung Djalan turned towards a leather sack and scooped from it the clearest kumiss, which he then poured into silver-mounted birch-wood cups. Slowly and with deep reverence he raised cup after cup to his forehead, and then sprinkled a few drops of the contents on the altar and the fire, paying due homage to the gods in words.

Not a single word was spoken; only the greedy smacking of the men's lips was heard, while the steaming bears' meat was laid on a dish which two young men then placed before Naidung Djalan. The smell of food was unendurable. All the men had drawn their long knives, and their eyes hung on every one of the host's movements.

At last he had cut up the meat into big lumps, which were distributed among the company. We ate, and we drank, and it was wonderful to satisfy our hunger with good, well-cooked food. The only people who seemed to preserve their

self-control were blind Bantje and his young guide. Surong was certainly eager to get good helpings, but he gave Bantje all the best pieces, and only when the old man was provided for did he himself eat what was left.

After the orgy of eating we crept back to the warm skin of the tent walls to make ourselves comfortable. And then came the many questions about the new conditions down on the steppe, and the answers, which gave rise to much reflection. Last of all the turn of the old songs came.

First Sangerup played and sang one of the steppe's oldest songs:

STEPPE POETRY

Under Father Jenghiz Khan's government the Mongols were well known
near and far and everywhere. Because he proclaimed the true law, he was named Bogdo—divinity.
They gave him the name Ikhe Bator, Great Hero, and the power in this name
can still to-day carry away us Mongols.
The peaks of a great mountain are very beautiful.
When one drinks water from this lake, one feels strength come to one.
When we remember our ancestors, we like to doze a little to be able to think much.
The great unchangeable father Khasar carried out well the gods' will.
He sacrificed many Mongols, but crushed even more enemies.
This effort cost the Mongols much strength, and they grew tired.
We Mongols, are we good, are we famous in the world ?
We must all honour our father Jenghiz and long for his return.

Surong had laid the stringed instrument on old Bantje's knee. Just for a moment the old man sat playing with its strings, to find the tune he wanted ; then he sang—an echo of Jenghiz Khan's ancient philosophy of life :

If a man leads a bad life, what shall one say of such a man ?
They who meet him are scorned and derided.
To an old friend and a bad man he is equally cruel.
If he sees something beautiful, he speaks indifferently.
He insults the poor and the low, and follows evil ways,
If he will gain advantages, he speaks softly and constrains himself.
But afterwards he turns away and acts ill.
Invite not such a man. Ignore such a man, for he is bad. . .
The high gods always show the way which leads to happiness.

A moment's silence, and then Bantje felt the strings afresh and broke into a new tune. His words were still instructive :

STEPPE POETRY

Of what use are women, who clothe themselves in five layers
of rich silk, but who are not worthy of a garment of leather?
If you have ten brothers, they cannot love you more than one father.
If you have ten layers of silk, they cannot outweigh one layer of wool.
If you have five sisters, they cannot love you more than one mother.
A warm fur coat, however bad it be, is useful when it grows cold.
A woman who does not love her husband in her youth becomes later
quite indifferent, but a fur coat is necessary in bitter cold.
A woman, whatever she looks like, becomes useful later.
In autumn the flower loses its beauty; when men and women are young
they love one another, in their older years they have forgotten everything.

The young women of the camp had finished their evening duties in the various tents, and now they came gliding in to take modest places at the entrance to the guest tent. Most of them were young, proud desert mothers, but there were also a few mature girls who would soon have their long plaits put up like those of the married women.

Naidung's eldest son sought out one of them with his eyes, and sang:

High up among the mountains grows a red flower; the splendid
  colour reminds me of all that is beautiful; very beautiful is the
  girl Bomberdi.
She stands out among a thousand for her beauty and wisdom.
Bomberdi, if I lose thee, how can I go on living?
If I lose thee to another, can I then live?

At last the fire sank to a glow, and the men began to knock out their pipes. In us too the fire had gone out, and the tent was emptied of its guests. At last we sat alone with Naidung Djalan and his sons.

The chief woman of the camp came in to clear up after the feast, but when she had done her work she remained sitting by the fire. She began to question Bantje cautiously about his journeys since they had last met, and her questions took him rapidly through the country of the Sunit and Chahar tribes. When he came to the Tumet country in his narrative, she became silent and exchanged glances with her husband and her sons.

At last she plucked up courage to put the question—had Bantje visited Haisan's camp on Lake Hangan? Had he brought any message from Shur-tsisik, their daughter and

sister, the little coral flower, whom two years ago they had given in marriage to the distant Tumet country?

Yes, Bantje had met the coral flower, and she was well and happy, but she had not forgotten her home camp in the Hsingan mountains. The coral flower had given him a message to take to her mother, and while the blind man sang this, tears of joy and sorrow streamed down the mother's cheeks—and also those of the three tough hunters.

STEPPE POETRY

Far away the married girl sits and longs for her mother.
Round Lake Hangan goes a pheasant singing.
We shall take wood from the apple-tree and make a cradle.
Summer comes, oh mother, with scents and colours.
Three months—and summer is over.
I long for the autumn, with alternate clouds and sunshine.
The grass becomes hay.
Three months—and the autumn is past.
I still long.
Spring comes, oh mother—the steppe changes colour.
In the cradle in my tent lies a beating heart.
The little bird of evening, oh mother, follows the sun's course over the hills, when I think of thee.

THE YOUNGER GENERATION OF MONGOLIA

A MONGOLIAN folk-song tells how, when Jenghiz Khan was born, the famous magician Hugtjo Bo stood at the mother's side to exorcise all evil spirits in the hour of birth.

Hugtjo Bo had foretold the time when the Mongols would be a great people under Jenghiz's leadership, and as a sign of the child's greatness the magician had had him placed in a cradle made like a chief's throne. Thence the new-born babe, in a sitting position, had begun at once to look out over the tracts of country he was later to dominate.

It is difficult to imagine how the world would have developed from the end of the twelfth century if Jenghiz Khan had not been born. But we know what his epoch brought with it and what its consequences were. From the unknown world of inner Asia the invincible Mongol horsemen broke out with a dynamic force which crushed all resistance.

THE YOUNGER GENERATION OF MONGOLIA

We all know that " the grass withered when Jenghiz Khan's horsemen galloped by "; but we are inclined to forget that the Mongols first brought the western world into contact with remote Peking. It was undoubtedly the Mongols who introduced much of the advanced culture of old China into our world. The art of printing books, which in its primitive form was a Chinese invention, is one of the cultural gifts the Mongols brought us.

During the long periods when the Mongols' men fit to bear arms were on the war-path between Asia and Europe, the steppe camps at home were ruled by women, and the Mongolian lads quickly became accustomed to discharge men's tasks. At an early age they had to swing themselves into the saddle to defend the camp's herds of cattle with bow and arrow against the wild beasts of the steppe.

When the warriors returned home for a short time between their battles, they told the camp lads of all those things to which young men most aspire, and every time the hordes set out to march towards distant frontiers, new legions of fighting men accompanied them.

" Those who come after me ", Jenghiz Khan said a short time before his death, " will deck themselves with jewels and brocade, they will enjoy foreign delicacies and costly wines, they will make love to beautiful young women—but they will forget the men and the life which are the origin of their riches. . . . And when the time comes, they will lose all I have given them, they will be hurled back into the desert where I found them, and they will wait long and in vain for a new Jenghiz Khan."

The old warrior and statesman was right in this prophecy as in so many others. When Jenghiz's descendants transferred the centre of Mongol power from the camp in the Khara Korum to the palace at Peking—when the Mongol governors and generals, who governed the distant possessions of the giant empire, adopted foreign customs and views, the qualities which had given them the mastery were gradually undermined. And when the Mongol leaders abandoned the tolerant attitude towards religion and the philosophy of life which had been Jenghiz Khan's greatest qualities, and adopted the fanatical religious views of the governing caste, the force which gave cohesion to the whole structure was broken and the Mongol empire dissolved.

As early as 1368 the Mongols were driven out of China, and the hordes rode back to the steppes from which Jenghiz Khan had led their forefathers.

But long after the nomads had exhausted their primitive strength, the large part of the Mongol race which had found its way back to its native steppes remained an incalculable danger to the peoples who lived around it. For Jenghiz Khan's injunctions were still the law of the steppe, and when they resumed the hardy life of the steppe the nomads developed fresh strength. Whenever a strong chief appeared in one of the Mongol tribes, the nomads began to hammer at the Great Wall of China, and it became a custom for the emperors of China to secure peace by buying them off. It was only necessary for a new Jenghiz to be born, a leader with his gift for uniting the people and his political wisdom, for a new Mongol empire to arise.

But then Indian Buddhism, in the disguise of Lamaism, came *via* Tibet to Mongolia, and this sealed the Mongols' fate for centuries. For Buddhism was able to subdue the elemental savage fury which had been the Mongols' strongest weapon.

For the Buddhist missionaries to be able to get a hearing for their pacific doctrine among the warlike Mongols, it was necessary to present it in a guise which was likely to be effective with the nomads, with their fidelity to tradition and love of mysticism. The numerous spirits and magicians of the old time were not condemned, but were converted and raised to positions of high dignity as " guardians " of the new religion.

The first Buddhist monastery in Mongolia was erected at the end of the sixteenth century, and the mystery and splendour which emanated from this new sanctuary—when combined with numerous miracles performed by its priests—quickly led to mass conversions among the Mongolian tribes. And the rulers of the neighbouring peoples, who saw in Lamaism an instrument with which they could suppress the Mongol danger once and for all, supported at great cost to themselves the propagation of the new doctrine on the steppes. Soon the desert was strewn with rich monasteries, from which innumerable priests preached the gospel of peace.

But at the beginning of the seventeenth century there were still enough pugnacious Mongols to take part with success in the campaign which drove out the Chinese Ming dynasty and set the Manchus on the Dragon Throne at Peking. From that day the Mongolian tribes placed themselves under the Manchu emperor's suzerainty and reckoned themselves as a part of China as long as this dynasty held sway.

In its early days, the time of its flowering, Lamaism had produced great thinkers and artists among the nomads, by nature so deeply philosophical, but in the course of years the good influence of the clergy became perverted. Monastery morals grew lax, the priests forgot their vows of chastity; thus venereal diseases began to spread among the population, and the total of births was catastrophically reduced.

At the end of the nineteenth century conditions on the steppes had become as degenerate as they are often described as being by Western travellers of modern times. Practically every single Mongol suffered from venereal disease. The education of children was conducted entirely in the unhealthy atmosphere of the monasteries, where indifferent priests taught uncomprehending disciples to gabble thoughtlessly the prayers which to their fathers had had a deep significance. The books used in the monastery schools were written in Tibetan, and the Mongolian written language was practically forgotten.

As more and more chiefs and highly-placed priests, who should have been the people's leaders, acquired a taste for the expensive luxury life of Peking, they—and with them the whole people—came into the power of Chinese money-lenders. To get money for themselves they sold fertile steppe land, and the Mongols' best pastures became Chinese agricultural land.

About 1910 what had once been the world's greatest nomad people was on the verge of ruin. If any remnants of the old love of liberty remained in the people, it must now rise and offer desperate resistance.

It was shown that the Mongols still had strength to fight, and the fall of the Manchu dynasty was the signal which lit the torches of freedom. Rebellion against the foreigners blazed up in 1912, when Northern Mongolia expelled all the Chinese garrisons stationed there. This liberation movement, which was strongly supported by Russia, soon spread to the other parts of the country ; but although the Mongolian arms were everywhere victorious, the rebellion led only to autonomy for Outer Mongolia, while the regions bordering on China became part of the new Chinese Republic.

In 1919—after the collapse of Tsarist Russia—China sent an army of 12,000 crack troops with modern equipment to Outer Mongolia, which they dominated for a short time, until Baron Ungern with his White Guard refugees came to the relief of the Mongols.

Two years later the Soviet Red Army invaded the country to destroy the last remnants of Admiral Kolchak's White Guard, and from that day Outer Mongolia, with its 600,000 inhabitants, has been an autonomous state in alliance with the Soviet Union and governed according to Soviet principles.

It is difficult to speak of the present state of things in this part of Mongolia, for since 1927 no non-Russian Westerner has been able to get permission to cross its frontiers. But it is said that conditions have improved in many respects. The old monasteries have been almost exterminated ; school attendance has been made compulsory ; venereal diseases— which had affected practically everyone—are said to have diminished in extent so greatly that they now affect only 26 per cent. of the population.

THE YOUNGER GENERATION OF MONGOLIA

When Japan, in 1931, occupied Manchuria to set up Manchukuo, all the eastern tribes of Mongolia, or about a million and a half Mongols, came under her control. These Eastern Mongolians, who had previously been in the power of the Manchurian marshals, had suffered from the Chinese colonization policy more than any other section of the population. Once they had been free, rich nomads; now, in the course of a generation, they had been impoverished and compelled to seek shelter in the remotest and poorest corners of their own country.

The Mongols would have welcomed and applauded any invasion which might overthrow the military power of China in their country, and at the beginning the Japanese move was received with enthusiasm by a great number of the young people.

When I set out in 1936 to investigate the remains of the once so powerful Eastern Mongolian horde, my first and foremost duty was to collect as many as possible of the old-time memories which were still preserved, before they disappeared without trace. I therefore visited the most out-of-the-way camps and their oldest inhabitants and lived with them for six wonderful months.

But when I returned, the young people had made an overpowering impression on me. I had met a generation whose overflowing energy and purposefulness gave me the first idea of a new future for the Mongols.

All the tribes of Eastern Mongolia have been united in the autonomous Hsingan-Mongolia. The head of this new Mongolian state is a Mongol of an old line of chiefs, but the Emperor of Manchukuo is his direct suzerain. The Mongols have their own army and their own police, and all the offices of state have been occupied by Mongols, but the men at the top have Japanese advisers.

Three hundred and fourteen schools have been established in the country, and Mongolian, ousted for centuries by Tibetan and Chinese, has again become the official written language.

Compulsory school attendance has been introduced, which prevents the monasteries from getting new disciples. All the young people I met between the ages of ten and seventeen could read and write Mongolian, and in the monasteries I visited I found on an average only half a dozen disciples under twenty.

I asked many of the leaders, and the young people who soon would decide the country's fate, about their view of religion ; and the gist of their answers was that in their eyes the gods were great and mighty now as they had been before, but that the priests had served them badly and thereby caused the misfortunes of the era now vanished.

But one could not lay hands on the representatives of the gods, however incapable they might be ; the priests, therefore, must be allowed to live out their lives as best they could, but they must be prevented from having any influence on the young. When the priests of the old era were dead, the gods would have new servants on earth—servants more worthy of them. Many young Mongols were already in Japan studying in the Buddhist monasteries, for it was clear that the gods must be served to their complete satisfaction in a country they so greatly favoured.

Everywhere I received the impression that in the world of religion two epoch-making changes were coming, which would completely remodel the Central Asiatic world by transferring the centre of Lamaism from Lhasa—under British influence— to the heart of Japan.

In several monasteries I met Buddhist priests, busily engaged in reshaping the principles of Lamaism in accordance with the ideas of the new doctrine. It is to be a religion which reveres the name of Buddha, but which does not condemn the shedding of blood, and in which the most direct road to eternal blessedness is a hero's death.

The last part of my journey in Eastern Mongolia was spent among a little community of nomad families who had their tents along the Buir-nor. In none of their camps did I meet any young men, and I saw only a few isolated children, all under seven. But there was no lack of labour, for the little remnant of the tribe which lived on the Buir-nor had long been poor, and its flocks of sheep and goats were so small that the old men could easily look after them.

We often talked of the times when the tribe had been rich in young men, and when the steppe, now so dead, had been alive with thousands of horses and cattle. We talked of the old men's sons, who were now fighting for Mongolia's future on unknown battlefields, and of their sons' young sons, who were now living in the new school and endeavouring to become worthy of the freedom which their ancestors had won for them.

The new school was a low clay hut, looking over the clear lake and endless undulations of green steppe. I rode to it with one of the two teachers of the school. He was an old man, and had once been a chief's adviser. He came of a family which had saved from destruction a copy of Sanang Setsen's old Mongolian chronicles. For generations his family had spent the long winter evenings over these chronicles, reading of the deeds of the Mongols in times gone by.

We found the other teacher in the little schoolroom, lecturing to his pupils. He was young and full of zeal, determined that the future of the Mongols should be as brilliant as their past. He had been two years in Japan to learn how a people marches to victory, and now the two of them—the old man and the young man—were trying to use their common knowledge for the benefit of the eleven children who were the tribe's new generation.

The lads were dressed in a sort of cadet uniform with polished buttons, and I had to look closely at their clean washed faces to convince myself that they really were Mongols. They made not the slightest attempt to show that indifference to surprises by which Mongols usually set so much store; as soon as the lesson was over they flung themselves upon me with a stream of eager questions.

On one wall hung a map of the world, on which Japan was

surrounded by a sun whose rays spread over the whole of Asia. Together we looked for and found the area, not marked with any name, which represented Scandinavia, and while the young teacher zealously took notes, and the boys' eyes hung on my lips, I told them about my own world. Scandinavia grew big—four kingdoms plus a republic and all Greenland. When I had finished my talk, the old teacher went to the map—and now all Scandinavia plus Greenland, with the seas that lie between, is enclosed in a large blue circle on the wall map in the school on the Buir-nor.

There were no more lessons in the school that day, for the children had to sing to the visitor. The songs were new, their text and tunes inspired by the New Time, but I felt that they were rooted in the same mentality as the old-time folk-songs.

When I had said good-bye to the schoolchildren, I went with the two teachers to enjoy the ceremonial farewell tea. They lived in the same house, for the old man's daughter was the young man's wife. The young woman sat in a corner of the room singing beside a cradle which hung from the ceiling. Its bottom was bent at an angle so that it formed a kind of easy chair, and on its rocking seat sat a child of two peering curiously out of the little window, out over the blue lake, the green steppe and the distant mountains on the horizon—out over Mongolia.

"Why, he's sitting in a cradle like the one Hugtjo Bo made for Jenghiz Khan," I said to the men. They looked at one another and then at me; then the reply came from the boy's father:

"We know quite well that a cradle like this is considered unpractical and harmful for children of your people, and even if we Mongols are now trying to be like you in many ways, we must still hold fast to those things in our own old culture which have in the past been a blessing to us. A cradle like this was given to Jenghiz Khan, and from no other kind of cradle has there ever grown up so great a ruler as he."

I turned to the mother and asked her to resume the song

THE YOUNGER GENERATION OF MONGOLIA

she had broken off when we came in. She refused bashfully for a long time, until the two Mongols supported me in my efforts to persuade her.

When she had finished her song and was rocking the baby to sleep, the grandfather took up his stringed instrument. When I left he was singing one of the old steppe songs in time with the rocking of the cradle, and the youngest nomad was sleeping the sleep that would bring him strength and health.

CHRISTMAS NIGHT IN THE WILD

I HAVE spent many Christmas nights in the wild regions of Central Asia, but never two in the same place. It is as though the high mountain passes and the uninhabited deserts continually urged one on to new wanderings into the unknown, towards new dwellings and new men. And yet life in its main outlines is always the same in those parts, for man cannot live in the wild without being charmed and marked by its quiet and grandeur.

It is extraordinary how life in a natural state, among natural human beings, can transform many of the great problems of civilized existence into unimportant trifles, while at the same time it discloses the existence of values hitherto unnoticed. But if a man has once been born and has grown up in the West, he can never tear himself away completely

CHRISTMAS NIGHT IN THE WILD

from its influence, for there are hours when hazy dream-pictures and isolated recollections bring on the incurable pains of homesickness.

When Christmas approaches, you suddenly become interested in the calendar ; you are seized with a nervous fear lest Christmas Eve should slip by unnoticed ; and when Christmas has come, you wind up your watch. You listen to its ticking, calculate the distance from home and the difference in time, and in one night recall all the great Christmas memories of your boyhood.

On Christmas Eve, some years ago, I was at Hailar, a town with a railway station on the Manchurian-Siberian frontier. In Hailar and its surroundings one can still meet genuine descendants of the wild Solon, Shibchin and Bodaha tribes, who remember the number of tents in the camps and all the details of life in the wild regions that were effaced when Hailar came into existence less than forty years ago— when the Russians laid down their trans-Manchurian railway. It was splendid country, they say, rich in game and good grazing and a citadel of old traditions and all kinds of magic.

Now the children of the wild have sought new places of refuge in the deep forests of the Hsingan mountains ; but before doing so they fought the Tsar's Cossacks for many years, and several of the railway stations are called after chiefs who fell in the hopeless struggle against the advancing railway and the civilization it represented.

After the victory of Bolshevism in Siberia, Hailar was for many years one of the centres from which White Guard exiles planned campaigns, which never came to anything, against their lost fatherland ; until in 1929 the Soviet, in its pretended war against China, got their leaders killed and their organization dissolved.

After the Japanese occupation of Manchuria, Hailar became, in 1932, one of the Japanese Empire's strong points on its new front against Siberia, and the many block-houses

CHRISTMAS NIGHT IN THE WILD

which were once erected by the colonial administration of Imperial Russia were converted into barracks for Japanese *buchitos*.

To-day Hailar is a kind of seething metropolis in the midst of a world of rude desolation and icy cold, and the variegated appearance of the town and its mixed population are in complete harmony with its chequered history.

It was the 24th of December, and I was wandering about the streets and alleys of Hailar, keeping my eyes open all the time for a bit of Christmas atmosphere. I walked towards the southern edge of the town, where rose the concrete silhouettes of a modern town quarter, square masses of masonry against the blue line of a distant mountain chain on the horizon. I was suddenly stopped by a notice announcing in six different languages that I was approaching the Japanese administrative centre, and that I should be shot without further warning if I continued my walk in that direction.

I turned round and sauntered back to the original Russian quarter which is still Hailar's centre. The wide streets of the Cossack town were flanked by solid block-houses, so low that one could rest one's arms on the roofs. It is said that they were built by Siberian Cossacks who were accustomed to fifty degrees of frost; the houses lay half buried in the earth, and all the joins of the planks were fastened together with soft moss.

Everywhere the snow lay feet deep, and the Cossack town looked like the scene of a romantic Christmas story. From the many mud-walled chimneys columns of smoke, white as steam, rose perpendicularly into the windless, clear frosty air, and the sour pungent smell of dried dung, which is here used as fuel, tickled the nostrils pleasantly.

Outside every house in the Cossacks' street were posts as tall as a man, to which visitors could tether their horses. At one of these posts tethered horses stood packed as close as herrings, and from the house came the sound of a balalaika and men's bass singing.

Over the low entrance door of the house were the words " Gotel Rim " (Hotel Rome). I went down and in, full of hopeful anticipation.

The interior of the house was filled by one large, half-dark room. Round a few round tables, on which mutton and bottles of vodka were laid out, a party of loud-voiced men were assembled. Most of them wore the wide sky-blue trousers with orange stripes which were part of the Trans-Baikal Cossacks' uniform, and they all had the big lock of hair on their foreheads, which was the distinguishing mark of these warriors. They had fought countless battles in the name of the White Tsar ; many of them still wore the Andrew Cross, the distinction for bravery, and Orthodox crucifixes on their hairy breasts, but their vodka-inflamed faces were as dark as those of Asiatics ; they swore and sang in Tartar, and they were now the Mikado's mercenaries.

I went over to the party, who made room for me in a hospitable, friendly manner, and I tried to feel at home. They offered me vodka, mutton, bread and salt, but I was not able to catch their mood. I pointed inquiringly at the chest of one of the Cossacks, where a shining brass Virgin and a black Shaman amulet dangled side by side.

" I got the yellow one from my Russian mother, the black one from my Tungan father ; and the black one has come out on top," he explained to me, grinning.

I rose to make room for a newly-arrived Cossack and slunk out again into the white snow and ringing frost.

Suddenly I heard a pleasant greeting in Russian, and when I turned round I saw in front of the Cossack tavern a sleigh whose three horses were covered with frozen pearls of sweat, glittering in the sun. A woman sat huddled up in the sleigh. She was wrapped in a large Asiatic fur, but her eyes were of a northern blue. When I gave her my Christmas good wishes in Russian, she turned with a scared air towards the noise from the Cossack tavern, and when I met her blue eyes again they were full of tears. " The Saviour has forsaken us poor souls," she whispered.

She pointed to a cupola on the edge of the Cossack town, over which a Byzantine cross danced like a mirage in the frosty air. " God's house lies desolate and forsaken, and no one rings the festival in with the bells which were brought from my holy Russia," she said. Then she sank back into the apathetic trance out of which my European face had drawn her for a few short moments, obediently awaiting the return of her Asiatic master.

I walked on towards the western edge of the town and passed a Lamaist temple, from whose dark interior the drone of drums and the priests' monotonous intoning rose and fell like echoes from a heathen inferno.

I sauntered back to the Cossack town and into the street which was inhabited by the Mohammedan Kazan Cossacks. The Mohammedan Cossacks were apparently more capable and more enterprising than their pseudo-Christian brothers in arms. Their houses were both larger and better kept, and most of them had both stables and large cattle-pens. Towards the end of the street lay their mosque, in a grove of twisted poplar trees, from which a slim shining white minaret pointed skywards.

A mullah wearing a turban appeared on the balcony of the minaret, whence he carefully observed the position of the sun and all the surrounding landscape.

The sun's pale disc was approaching the jagged line of mountains on the south-western horizon ; it grew larger and turned red as it approached the snow-covered earth, and the whole landscape was filled with blue shadows, which swiftly darkened and increased in size.

From the steppe were heard the cracking of whips and loud cries from the boys and girls who were driving the cattle home. The doorways of all the yards in the street were opened wide, and young veiled women appeared to receive each her share of the lowing herd. Then the doorways were shut again; the whole street lay desolate and abandoned. *Namas*, the hour of prayer, was at hand.

The sun had disappeared behind the fringed silhouette of the mountain horizon. For a short time all the colours imaginable played in the south-western sky, before dusk spread over the landscape; and then the evening came on—Christmas Eve. Icy gusts of wind came sweeping down from the mountains, and I waded on hurriedly through the deep glistening snow of the streets.

I came into a new Japanese quarter and was attracted by a door on which large decorated paper lanterns hung. I went cautiously into the warmth, into a large tavern full of Japanese soldiers, who were squatting round low lacquered tables. Smiling geishas in gaily-coloured kimonos were tripping about among the tables to sweeten existence for their heroes, who had won this rude desolate country for their distant homeland.

They all ignored me without being uncivil in any way. I was to them just a foreigner who had no business whatever in this country, though I had travelled all over it before they had ever set foot there. I began to reflect on the absolute senselessness of my being frozen up among all these heathens on this day, Christmas Eve.

A pretty little geisha had taken a stringed instrument and to its hard accompaniment was singing a song which broke in sharply upon my thoughts of home.

I hurried out into the night, home to my quarters, filled with a wild desire for some Christmas atmosphere. I put my best pair of horses into the sledge, and soon I was in wild flight—away from Hailar with all its alien people and out over the soft endless snow of the steppes. The snow flew from the horses' galloping hooves and the sleigh's creaking runners, and the whole of the dark night sky was brilliant with stars.

CHRISTMAS NIGHT IN THE WILD

The night was so wonderful that it made my heart rejoice. It was icy cold, from the snowfields came a crackling like the liveliest firework display, and long shooting stars wrote glowing Christmas greetings between heaven and earth.

Now and then I had to stay my furious course to be able to order my thoughts and take stock of my surroundings.

I saw shepherds' fires here and there out on the steppe. The stillness of the night and the icy cold made the flames rise up like pillars, which in a twinkling tore themselves free from earth to form weird mirages among the stars—then they unfolded themselves like curtains of fire, before they sank down to earth again as just pale little fires lit by men's hands.

I had set my course towards the middle star of Orion's belt, but suddenly the horses began to move irregularly, toss their heads uneasily and turn away to southward. I peered out on both sides to discover the cause of their uneasiness, and found that I had on my right the edge of a low wood several hundred yards away. The wood was white with snow, so that it blended with the rest of the countryside, but seen from the racing sleigh its treetops looked like white ghosts slipping past the low stars of the horizon.

Suddenly the sledge gave a jerk; the horses reared and snorted with fear, and suddenly set off at a furious gallop, curving sharp to the left. Looking back, I saw points of light in pairs approaching from the edge of the wood. The wolves came nearer and nearer, and I peered into the darkness for a camp fire.

As the hours passed, the wolves became bolder and bolder; they gathered in parties and came nearer, and it gradually became almost impossible to manage the nervous horses. At last I gave them free rein, and we came up with a couple of shepherds who were trying, with loud cries, to keep an uneasy herd of horses inside the circle of fires which they had lighted to scare the wolves.

Now they were right upon us, and the herd of horses pressed

together in a compact mass, rocking and swaying to and fro, as all the horses tried to work their way as near the centre as possible. Three splendid stallions were circling outside the herd in wide curves ; most alarming they looked with their flung-up heads and bared teeth. Five grey wolves attempted an attack, but the stallions were ready for them, biting at them with lowered heads, stamping with their fore-feet till the snow creaked, and kicking out behind after their agile assailants. The shepherds joined the fray with burning brands and flung these at the wolves, which gradually sneaked back into the darkness.

Then we moved off and at last reached the shepherds' camp. Although the night was far advanced, we found all the men on their legs and in full activity, for it was one of the nights when the children of nature have to fight against the powers of nature.

The wolves' boldness had driven all the young men out to the great flocks of sheep to keep the fires alive and the beasts at a distance ; and the young women were fully occupied bringing in the newly-born lambs, which the pregnant sheep were dropping on account of the severe cold, to the warm tent fires. The children and old men were running round trying to quiet the horses, while the old women and the oldest men were occupied inside the tents warming the lambs which had been brought in and keeping the great pots of tea on the boil.

I took my horses out of the sleigh, rubbed them dry and quieted them with words and caresses. Then I went into the chief tent of the camp, whose headman, with dignified friendliness, offered me the guest's place on the right of the altar. He offered me tea and cheese, and we exchanged politenesses. When we had got to know all we needed to know about each other, we sat down comfortably to sip tea and smoke tobacco and exchange pleasant chat.

The smiling, dignified Djirimtai betrayed now and again that his senses were on the alert ; he heard all the noises from

CHRISTMAS NIGHT IN THE WILD

the steppe and understood what they meant; he directed the women who came in carrying the new-born lambs, and from time to time he shouted curt orders to the shepherds outside.

Gradually the howling of the wolves died away, and peace returned to the camp. The women came back to their duties in the tents, the old men sought their warm corners in the tents again, and at last the young shepherds too came in. Everyone was happy and cheerful as after a successful party, and the dangerous episodes of the night were discussed as if they had been amusing experiences.

We ate, drank tea and exchanged tobacco, and everyone treated me with friendliness. They told me about their affairs and I told them about mine; our stories seemed to follow each other in natural, harmonious sequence. The old men had laid down to sleep already; the fire was dying down, and the young people's talk had become as soft as a caress. A couple of instruments were taken down from their places on the tent wall and reached the hands of two young shepherds, who played and sang the song " Comrades' Thoughts "

The camp fire was now a heap of smoking embers; darkness enveloped the tent, and the tea-pot had gone off the boil. A circular patch of stars shone in through the round vent and was reflected in the tea in my flat wooden cup. I felt that I was sitting with a whole star-strewn sky in the hollow of my hands.

I looked at my watch: two in the morning by local Japanese time, so it was 6 p.m. the day before by Central European time. The Christmas bells were ringing now at home in Scandinavia, and the Christmas trees would soon be lit up.

Around I heard the sound sleep of the satisfied children of nature and the light breathing of the newly-born lambs. I played with my cup till I had got a big Christmas star right in the middle of the black surface of tea, and then I drained it to the bottom.

One of the shepherds came in from the steppe to fetch his relief, and I crept into my sleeping-bag to dream my own dreams. But before the shepherd lay down to sleep he played one of the steppe tunes, and it sounded in my ears like the most delightful Christmas hymn.

THE MONGOLS' "BLUE CITY"

THE history of the frontier regions along the Great Wall of China is a perpetual struggle between such contrasted interests as the savage hordes' desire for new lands and the nomads' need of virgin pastures.

The happiest chapters in the history of China and all Central Asia are the periods in which the emperor who sat on the Dragon Throne was powerful enough to make the Wall insuperable, and wise enough to open its gates to peaceful intercourse between the two so different worlds.

The broad valley, through which the snow-water runs from the tableland of Mongolia on its way to the Yellow River, forms a natural terminus for the caravan traffic that maintains communication between China and all the states which lie outside the Wall.

The town which on most maps of Asia is called Kwei Sui, and which is marked as chief town of the Chinese province of Sui-yuan, was originally named Khukhu Khoto. In 1936 this again became the town's official name, when it became capital of the newly established Meng-chiang-Mongolia.

Khukhu Khoto is Mongolian and means " the blue city ". The town bore this name in its most brilliant period, when it was the residence of the Tumet chieftains.

It was here that the famous Altan Khan, the " Golden Khan ", who was the Tumet Mongols' greatest leader, conceived his great plans ; from here he supervised their execution and administered his great dominions. It was from here that he threatened China's weak Ming emperors so that they had to pay dearly for his goodwill ; and from here that he sent out sages in search of the truth to the holy places of his distant Tibet, which contributed more than anything else to the conversion of the whole of Mongolia to Buddhism. The gold which the Ming emperors paid to Altan Khan as " Danegeld " he used for the erection of palaces, temples and monasteries, the roofs of which he encrusted with blue glazed stones.

Rumours of the town's splendour spread all over Central Asia ; the nomads who streamed to it, when from the top of the passes to the north they caught sight of the blue-gleaming beauty of all the curved roofs and slender pagodas, gave it the name Khukhu Khoto ; and the " blue city " became the background of many of Asia's legends and tales of adventure.

In the shadow of the pagodas the Golden Khan had schools built, where the Mongols who streamed to the city were instructed in the mysteries and dogmas of the new religion. He had the sacred books of Buddhism translated into Mongolian in the monasteries, and the Mongols who returned to their homes spread the books and the ideas of the new creed in their districts.

THE MONGOLS' "BLUE CITY"

Altan Khan's successors, however, were less vigorous than he himself had been ; and when the Chinese Ming dynasty had sunk so deep in degenerate impotence that the way to Peking lay open to a daring conqueror, it was not the Tumet Mongols, but their Manchurian kinsmen to the east, who seized power in China and set their own chieftain on the Dragon Throne.

The first Manchu emperors were both shrewd and bold, and they soon succeeded, by force or diplomacy, in making the whole of Central Asia dependent on the government at Peking.

The Manchus established a strong garrison in the neighbourhood of the " blue city ", and for this garrison, and for the officials who were to administer the conquered country, they built a quite new city with stately dwelling-houses and temples, surrounded by a massive crenelated wall.

Sui-yuan, " new city ", was its name. But as the whole administration of the surrounding region was concentrated within its walls, Sui-yuan gradually became the name for the province which had formerly been the free domain of the Tumet Mongols. Indeed, the farther towards north and west the Manchurian cavalry pushed the frontier of the Empire, the longer and more numerous became the caravan routes which led to and started from the valley where the " blue city " lay. To it came Buriats and Khalkha Mongols with their long-haired Bactrian camels laden with furs and scented musk ; Sarts and Kirgises, their long-legged dromedaries bearing precious metals, Khotan jade and glittering stones ; and Tungans whose beasts of burden were hardly visible under huge bales of the finest Sining wool.

And when the caravans had rested, they set out again on their long journeys through Mongolia to Siberia, Turkestan, Tibet and still more distant countries with valuable cargoes of silk, tea, tobacco, spices and other delicious Chinese products.

Between the two twin cities, the old Mongol city with its blue temple roofs and the new Manchu city with its high walls, in the course of time a whole new town sprang up : a town with bazaars fringed with *serais* for travellers, and with shops representing many of the great trading houses of Asia. As time passed the two neighbouring cities were swallowed up by this ever-growing merchant city, which had neither emperor nor Khan as its founder, but where Chinese, Muscovites and Central Asiatics, representing many races and religions, added house to house and street to street.

In the period of 250 years, for which the Manchus were able to keep the Great Wall an insuperable barrier between ploughed fields and open steppes, trade between China and Central Asia continued to flourish, and the population of Sui-yuan and many other places became rich and secure.

When the two and a half centuries were over, the Manchus had enjoyed wealth and prosperity for so long that their energy had flagged, and in 1912 it was again the turn of the Chinese to rule China. But the latter-day Chinese never mounted the Dragon Throne ; they were the champions of modern ideas, which resulted in the Chinese Republic. In accordance with the ideas of the new time, a little band of

Chinese were now to rule China's 400 millions as well as all the subject lands lying outside the Wall.

Tibet, Turkestan and Northern Mongolia made themselves independent of China before its new government had an opportunity of applying its reforming zeal to those isolated regions ; but it got to work in Inner Mongolia, just beyond the Great Wall, in 1928. The plan was that the lean steppes, which could hardly feed a million nomads, should be thrown open to 28 millions of Chinese peasants, and in the years that followed the nomads were driven steadily northward, farther and farther into the desert and poverty.

In 1934 conditions among the nomads were so desperate that they rose and offered armed resistance. In the years that followed the Mongols drove away all the Chinese colonists outside the Wall ; in 1937 a Mongolian chief again entered the Golden Khan's " blue city ", and Mongolian warriors are again riding through its streets. But these are Mongols who wear khaki uniforms and carry modern weapons, and they have no apparent connection with the people who once founded the city.

All the administrative officials, from the judge in the Yamen to the gendarmes in the streets, are Mongols, but they are swallowed up in the overwhelming Chinese street life that seethes around them. The narrow glittering alleys of the bazaars run into an absolutely straight street bounded by high walls. Huge acacias lean over them and throw dark shadows on the yellow dust of the street. Neither women nor children are to be seen, only bearded men all hurrying in the same direction without their tall figures losing dignity for a moment. At the end of the street a shining white minaret rises from the soft outlines of an acacia grove. Just below the top of the minaret hangs a narrow balcony ; a white-bearded old man appears on it. All the hurrying men put on speed, and I follow them into a large courtyard, where we mingle with a waiting crowd.

I see around me only men, bearded men, wearing long black

coats and on their heads high turbans of the whitest muslin. They all stand facing west, but their eyes seek the old man up in the white minaret and follow each of his movements. He also stands facing west, his fingers stroking his long white beard ; then he puts his hands to his ears, as though trying to catch a distant noise. The whole congregation at the foot of the minaret make the same gestures as the old man with a precision and dignity which show that they are performing a ceremony of deep religious significance.

Suddenly the silence is broken by a wolf-like howl. The whole congregation fall on their knees ; in this posture they continue their graceful movements of the hands and bend the upper part of their bodies far forward. The shrieks from the minaret balcony are repeated as a reminder to all the Mohammedans in the town of the one God who is theirs, of Allah's great prophet and of the distant home in which they have their roots. There follows the stereotyped confession of faith : " There is only one God, and Mohammed is his prophet."

The voices of children chanting by rote come from one of the side buildings of the mosque, and through an open window I see a dozen children singing the lesson for the day in chorus with shrill voices, and to a pleasant but endless tune. The children are of all ages from four to fourteen, and hold the holy Koran on the palms of their outstretched hands. The appearance of my face at the open window causes little quick side-glances from their black childish eyes ; but the atmosphere in the room is not disturbed, for their young minds must concentrate zealously to understand and retain the creed, the language and the writing which their ancestors generations ago brought to the " blue city " from their homeland in the far west.

THE MONGOLS' "BLUE CITY"

The Golden Khan and his Tumet Mongols who once built the " blue city "—and all the nomads whose tented camps, studs of horses and herds of cattle dotted the surrounding country in still earlier days—what has become of them ? Are no traces of their time of greatness to be found ?

Many travellers have come to Sui-yuan from the coast of China, have traded with the people of the district and walked in the streets of the town without acquiring the smallest idea of its past life.

But if you come from the north with one of the caravans bound for the " blue city ", and if you have listened to the immortal stories which long ago became current among the visiting nomads, impressed by the splendour of the place, then you go straight through the noisy bazaars till you come to the crumbling buildings which once were the heart of the Golden Khan's proud city.

There can be heard the mumbling, wailing, droning voices which ooze from the Golden Khan's ancient temples like echoes from a vanished time and a vanished world. And if you follow the sounds, you find in the light of the lotus-shaped butter lamps the yellow-robed priests, still sacrificing to the Golden Khan's gods, once so brilliant but now much the worse for wear.

But in one of the time-worn palaces craftsmen are at work restoring its earlier splendour. And the last conquerors of the city, the young and vigorous Mongols have pitched their tents in the shade of the trees that surround it. Here in the midst of his warriors lives Teh Wang, descendant of Jenghiz Khan and the country's new master. Here I met also the young chief of Abak, who broke through the Chinese defence lines, and many others in whose homes on the steppe I have often been a guest. And in the midst of these hardy, vigorous nomads sits the man who is chief of the remnants of the Tumet people, who for many years led a miserable existence of poverty and hardship, and whom the conquerors have now brought into the limelight.

With Teh Wang, whose name among friends and equals is Demchik Dorche, I ascended the five-spired tower of the temple city. This, the Golden Khan's proudest work, still rises above Mohammedan minarets, Chinese temples and

thousands of grey shop roofs. Our eyes wandered along the horizon, and Teh Wang talked till I too saw with his eyes. . .

From the passes to the north curved white stripes run down towards the centre of the old town. These are the beginning and the end of the roads which connect this place with every centre and out-of-the-way corner in Central Asia. Towards the southern horizon one can just see the old Wall of China.

THE MONGOLS' "BLUE CITY"

It runs eastward and westward as far as the eye can reach, like a blood-red memorial of ineradicable mistrust between cunning peasants and tough nomads.

And over to westward the waters of the Yellow River roar down like a noisy overture till they come to the barren Ordos desert. Deep in this desert lies Etsin Horo, " the possessor's enclosure ", with the camp of the Great Khan. It is fanatically protected by descendants of Jenghiz Khan's proud bodyguard. They are all " white-boned " (noble), but no marks of distinction have been worn in their hats since the day, more than seven centuries ago, when their ancestors took them out as a sign of mourning for their great master's death.

For more than seven hundred years generation after generation of the old bodyguard's successors have watched over the tents which contain the Great Khan's weapons and other relics. Through century after century Mongolian noblemen, descendants of Jenghiz Khan, who still govern the Mongol tribes, have flocked from every district of Mongolia to the great annual sacrificial feasts at the Great Khan's sarcophagus.

Mongols will tell you that in the main tent at Etsin Horo there is a silver chest which holds the remains of the great Jenghiz. Other Mongols declare that the silver chest is inside an iron chest ; others again, that within the silver chest there is a gold chest. Indeed, the farther one gets from Etsin Horo, the more numerous and more costly the chests become which, the Mongols say, enclose the remains of their great leader. All the nomads of Mongolia hope and believe that the day will come when the deified chieftain will rise up from his sarcophagus to lead his chosen people to a new era of greatness. And when that day comes, the guard at Etsin Horo will again set precious stones and peacock feathers in their chiefs' hats, and, on snow-white horses, will follow their ruler on new rides over the eternal steppes of Mongolia.

I myself have stood at Etsin Horo—but I resisted the temptation to reveal its secret.

Ought not we, who live so far from the silent desert world

of Ordos, to believe its most beautiful legend—and long for the day when we can set the sparkling jewel of adventure and the gay peacock's feathers of imagination in our everyday hats?

WITH FIRE-WORSHIPPERS IN MONGOLIA

IF one turns to literature, handbooks and classical travel descriptions of past times, one learns that fire, in its capacity as one of the five elements, the child of wood, mother to the earth and enemy of all the metals, plays a very important part in several of Asia's ancient religions. One can read of travellers in Central Asia who have displeased their hosts by throwing cut-off nails, hair and other " unclean " things on to the fire or by putting their feet against the hearth. One finds that Marco Polo had heard of three places in Persia which were inhabited by fire-worshippers. The legend ran that the three holy kings of the Bible set out from those places to find out whether the reports of the new-born Saviour were true. Each of them took with him his special gift, which should be an offering to the new-born Messiah and at the same time should prove whether the child were a Divine Saviour or not. If he preferred gold, he was only an earthly king ; if he held out his hand for myrrh, he was a worker of miracles ; but if he chose incense, the kinsman of fire, that was a proof that he was the real Saviour. The Christ-child accepted all three offerings, and in return he presented to the three kings a stone; this later on was miraculously transformed into a fire, whose flames have been nourished through the centuries by the Persian fire-worshippers.

But in all the accessible literature the seeker after knowledge finds very little which can help him to understand the mystical " fire customs " of the grey felt tent and their dark meaning in the Central Asia of our days.

When one begins to travel in Mongolia a strong feeling of well-being comes over one. The healthy life in saddle and tent; the immense loneliness, unknown to a Westerner, in which one never feels lonely; the dignified friendliness and complete reliability of the inhabitants—all these make one feel in harmony with one's surroundings. The mysticism which surrounds one creates an atmosphere of romance, which everyone interprets in his own way. What a man feels first and foremost is that he is living through all the healthiest dreams of his boyhood, dreams of which the artificial life of civilization long ago deprived him.

But if you travel long enough and learn as the days pass, you begin to understand that behind the nomad's mysticism lies more than a casual momentary sentimentalism, that all the things which are apparently fortuitous are significant, determining factors in the nomads' life—that all you yourself sense only faintly is the outward expression of a force which leads the nomads from the cradle to the grave and on to heaven —which protects family life, holds the clan together and orders the history of the tribes. It is this mysterious force which upholds morality, law and order in a country in which there are no police and no professional judges.

The hearth is the natural centre in all the tents of Mongolia, and it may well be said that despite the nomads' hardy out-of-doors existence, the tent fire is the most important factor in their lives. All food and drink is cooked and heated over the camp fires; they are the tents' only source of warmth in the long, cold winters ; in their light the people collect in the evenings to work and to make themselves comfortable after the lonely, tiring journeyings of the day. But for the warmth of the fires a great part of the young of the herds and flocks would be lost, for all the prematurely born lambs and calves, which now spend their first night in the warm south-west corner of a tent, would freeze to death if relegated to the inclement steppe.

It is round the camp fires of an evening that these hard-living men's experiences are related, take shape and are passed on with the natural man's strongly developed sense of the dramatic, till they acquire the fantastic form of a popular legend without ever losing touch with reality. And it is by the flaming fires in the assembly tents of the camp that the deeds of ancestors are related and sung, that the nomads' old tunes and legends are kept alive and handed on to the new generation.

The reverent listener feels that he is only an arm's length from a milieu which has its roots far back in the earliest years of the country and its inhabitants.

The Mongolian hearth consists of a four-sided block of wood, in the middle of which an iron " four-foot " forms the actual fireplace. This " four-foot " consists of four perpendicular iron legs, held together by four horizontal iron rings. The tops of the iron legs are shaped like curved birds' beaks, and on them pots and pans of different sizes can be hung. The practical function of the four iron rings is to keep together the burning camel- and horse-dung which is the fuel most used by the Mongols.

Like everything else on which the Mongol has laid his hands or cast his eyes, the fireplace has its legend ; but it is notable that, although he regards it with great reverence, the legend of the " four-foot " is one which symbolizes hostility to the nomad's way of life and all the ideals by which he sets most store.

WITH FIRE-WORSHIPPERS IN MONGOLIA

The Mongols themselves declare that in their time of greatness these four-legged iron fireplaces were not used; in those days the fire was lighted inside a circle of stones, collected in the neighbourhood of the camp fire.

If the Mongols are asked when the four-footed iron fireplace 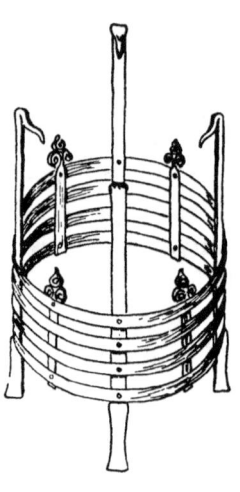 was introduced, they explain that it coincided with the end of their time of greatness; and if they consider the questioner worthy of greater confidence, they will tell him that the one thing was a consequence of the other, because the fireplace was imposed on them by their new Chinese masters. The iron fireplace, which has now for centuries been the centre of the sacred hearth in all the tents of Mongolia, possesses magic power. Its horizontal iron rings bind the nomads to the place where they live, and prevent them from setting out on distant wanderings; and the beak-shaped tops of the four legs symbolize vultures, which watch over all the great thoughts, inspirations and ideals which spring to life in the fire of the hearth, and suppress them before they have found their way into the Mongols' hearts.

The hearer may express his astonishment that, this being so, the Mongols use the four-footed iron fireplaces and do not return to the old fire of stones; but here he comes up against the nomads' fatalistic view of life. They will tell him that an inimical power rules in Mongolia and must be obeyed until heaven some day sends them a new Jenghiz Khan, who will be able to free them.

The chief woman of the tent has her place at the south-eastern corner of the hearth. From here she looks after the fire and discharges all her duties as housewife and hostess. This is her rightful place and is inviolable; so long as she occupies it she has unrestricted freedom of speech and action.

She can use whatever words she likes, and can even with impunity throw pokers and bones at guests who displease her, and at inhabitants of the tent. But if she gives up her seat she can be called to account for what she does, and she may never pass the north-western corner of the tent, for this is the sacred place of the Lamaist altar. She can approach it from one side or from the other, but she may never pass in front of it.

The visitor learns by his own observation, without receiving any admonition or instruction in words, that the pleasant companionship round the camp fire of an evening is subject to a strict etiquette, and that any breach of this immediately destroys the harmony and peaceful atmosphere of the gathering. He acquires too with time a practical knowledge of the most important " fire customs ". The consequence of this is that the polite reserve of the nomads disappears, and one begins to feel one's way forward towards an understanding of the real background of camp etiquette. But only when he has got thus far is he found worthy of a more intimate confidence and allowed to be present at the celebrations and sacrificial feasts, which reveal the object and meaning of the Mongol creed.

Fire is the dwelling-place of a divinity, and is in itself a divinity. It is for fear of insulting the divinity of the hearth that one may not throw nails, hair and other " unclean " things on the fire.

There are elements in the creed which indicate that in an earlier stage at any rate it was connected with the worship of the sun.

Besides the fire divinity himself, who is called the " fire king " or " youngest brother ", there are in the fire seven maidens. Their faces are blinding white, their teeth like white mother-of-pearl, their eyebrows of turquoise ; they hold pearl axes in their hands, and wear crystal belts about their loins. Of the fire-god's appearance, they say that he is dark red ; he takes the shape of a flame, and his heat has the power to penetrate the earth-god's seventy-seven heavens.

WITH FIRE-WORSHIPPERS IN MONGOLIA

Of the origin of fire, the ritual tells that it was lighted by the mighty Jenghiz Khan, blown to a flame by Torgon Sjare, who saved Jenghiz Khan's life, and preserved by Jenghiz Khan's wife.

A great sacrificial feast in honour of the fire-god is held once a year in all the tents of Mongolia—on the twenty-third day in the Mongols' twelfth month.

In one of the camps of the Adochen people Sjagder was headman. He and I had once ridden in the same caravan across the steppes of Mongolia, the Gobi sand desert, the oases of Turkestan and the barren mountains of Tibet.

For a week or two we had been reviving our memories of those days—all that we alone in this camp had in common, all that we alone could talk of, and all the great experiences and adventures in distant lands, strange to us both, which bound us together in a sort of kinship which was stronger than many a blood relationship. I realized that if I ever was to have a chance of being present at the great sacrificial feast in the fire-god's honour, it must be here in Sjagder's tent. Permission was given as a quite natural thing.

On the morning of the 23rd the young men of the camp rode to the Chinese merchants to make purchases, while the women of the camp did the necessary cleaning-up in their respective tents. Everywhere the fire had been allowed to go out, and fireplaces, smoke-vents and tent altars made clean and bright.

I sat out by the sheep-folds with Sjagder and other leading men of the camp and watched some shepherds choosing and slaughtering the sheep which were to be sacrificed in the evening. They cut from each sheep the breast-bone, four ribs, two knee-bones and some of the fat surrounding the liver. These parts constituted the blood offering ; they were laid on wooden dishes and carried out to the respective tents.

It was nearly sunset. The inhabitants of the camp disappeared into their tents to put on their finest attire in freezing cold by the feeble light of a butter lamp.

In Sjagder's tent lived the headman himself, his old wife, a son of sixteen and an unmarried daughter with two small children. An old uncle, who had once held chieftain's rank, not inheritable, for his great ability and knowledge, and two married sons who lived in other tents in the camp, had come to participate in the sacrificial ceremony.

The old uncle was as a matter of course *medek hung* of the tent—i.e. the person who reads the traditional ritual service and directs the course of the sacrifice. For this purpose he was placed in front of the tent altar in the north-western corner and facing the hearth. Before him stood a low sacrificial table, on which the necessary ingredients were laid.

I was allotted a place to the left of the old *medek hung*, between Sjagder and his married sons, and to our left, between Sjagder's youngest married son and the entrance to the tent, sat his wife and his two daughters-in-law. By the western wall of the tent, between the *medek hung* and the entrance, were Sjagder's unmarried daughter with her two children and his son of sixteen.

We all sat in an almost complete circle ; the only opening was the place between the entrance to the tent and the hearth, where the bloody skin of the sacrificial animal lay on the ground.

For a little while we sat silent and expectant ; the eyes of all were turned in eager anticipation on the old *medek hung*, who slowly and thoroughly examined the offerings that lay before him. He gave a sign, on which the youngest son of the tent snatched an old blunderbuss from the tent wall and dashed out on to the steppe ; four shots rang out and echoed in the cold night, and the camp dogs set up a furious barking, as if they wanted to do their part in driving away all evil spirits from the impending ceremony.

The chief woman of the tent (Sjagder's wife) received from the *medek hung* a bundle of sticks and laid them carefully in the middle of the hearth. Next she heaped up sun-dried manure along the inner sides of the fireplace. All eyes were fixed upon her hands while she slowly and cautiously lit the fire, and in breathless excitement all watched the first puffs of smoke curling up towards the smoke-vent, to make out their shape and colour. To the joy of all they quickly became bright and light and rose like a morning mist under the sun's rays.

The *medek hung* lit four sticks of incense and handed them one by one to Sjagder, who passed them on to me. When they had gone round the circle four times they were placed in the four corners of the hearth. The fire was now blazing up brightly and cheerfully and was spreading warmth and light in the tent, previously so cold and dark, while the incense filled the air with a pleasant sweetness.

While the chief woman was fastening to the points of the fireplace narrow strips of cloth in the colours of the dawn, the midday sun, twilight and night, the *medek hung* took the great sacrificial dish and threw the choicest bits on the fire, uttering as he did so the old tent ritual :

> Thou who spreadest smoke, who can pierce through the clouds,
> Thou who hast a heat which can pierce through Mother Earth,
> Thou, lighted by the mighty Jenghiz Khan,
> Thou, nourished by the mighty Torgon Sjare,
> Thou, kept alive by the mighty chief woman,
> come to our tent.

The *medek hung* handed the sacrificial dish to Sjagder, who raised it to his forehead and descended from his place of honour to the entrance. Here he took up his stand on the outspread sheepskin, facing the fire. The *medek hung* continued the old ritual, handing to the chief woman, as he did so, a bowl of brandy and butter :

The fire-stone came from the mountains,
the leather from a good man.
Darkhan the smith bound the fire-box with steel,
and mighty Jenghiz Khan struck the steel.
Crackling flowed the seven-tongued fire,
and the mighty chief woman laid it on our hearths.

Sjagder bent low with the heavily loaded sacrificial dish, and then committed to the flames its contents of flesh, bones and blood. For a brief moment the flames paled under the juicy load, but the chief woman flung lump after lump of yellow butter into the middle of the fire and poured brandy over it, till the flames, crackling and throwing sparks, rose high and issued through the smoke-vent. The smell of burnt flesh and charred bones mingled with that of incense ; shadows and huge coloured flames flickered and shifted within the tent walls; and the excited, perspiring faces of those who sat round shone bright in the weird illumination.

Through the crackling of the flames the old man's voice, repeating the ritual, was heard:

Thou fire, who camest to us, when the mountains were but hillocks,
when the brown he-goat was a kid,
when the trees were twigs,
Thou, whose lot is as a mighty ruler's,
accept our sacrifice.

The violent blaze of the fire slowly died down into quiet, steady flames and then into embers. All sat bent forward towards the fire and eagerly noted the changes in its shape, colour and smell. Now and then they glanced at the old *medek hung's* face, which slowly became less strained, was smoothed out, and at last bore the marks of intense relief. The last flames sank back into the embers, where the last remnants of the sacrifice were melting and vanishing.

The old man leaned back against his raised seat with a sigh of contentment and announced with a smile, which drew cries of delight from all:

The new fire on the hearth is happily lighted;
The fire-god of this hearth is pleased with our sacrifice,
and the divine fire maidens of the world's four quarters have again
                                      taken up their abode there
and will watch over this tent's future.

These words caused an outburst of delirious joy in Sjagder's tent. The chief woman resumed her place at the south-eastern corner of the hearth, whence she laid more fuel on the fire for the preparation of the festal meal.

The old musical instruments were taken down from their hooks; Sjagder poured brandy into a jug and served the company liberally, having first given the fire, the smoke-vent, and the four quarters of the globe their share. The festal mood was exalted and prolonged, with food and wine, song and legend, and memories of ancient gods and ancient times.

THE HOLY FIRE MAIDEN

IT was in the eleventh month of the year of the Fire Tiger (1926) that I met Djalserai and Jetom in the temple city of Mundy. They had come to pay their clan's annual tribute of costly furs to the " Living Buddha ", who lived there ; I to have a good rest after a summer of tiring travel.

Djalserai and Jetom were brothers and sons of old Demchik, who long years before had been my caravan leader on a long journey through the mysterious countries of Central Asia. The family belonged to a Buriat tribe, and his clan was renowned ; for generations it had produced some of the most famous hunters in the Altai mountains.

It was easy to see that the two brothers were related ; but, young as they were, they already bore the different stamps of the ways of life which God had marked out for them. Djalserai was a hunter, and had acquired the active gait, the quick movements and the searching glance of the tracker. Jetom was a lama, and twenty-three years in a monastery had long ago lulled to sleep his inherited instincts. He had become a pallid bookworm, and the only heights his short-sighted eyes now sought were those to which a study of the holy books could raise him.

We had a great deal to talk about, and I understood from

the two young Buriats that the adventures I had had in distant countries in their old father's company were both fertile and favourite subjects of conversation by the hearths at home. I was seized by an uncontrollable longing to see again my friend of those long journeys and hear him tell in his fashion of things which I remembered in my own way.

On the seventeenth day of our journey we sighted the peaks of the Altai mountains, sparkling with glaciers, and six days later we rode from the steppe into the snow-white kingdom of the " Mountains of Gold ". It was years since I had seen woods, and now I was riding for days on end through narrow valleys, whose slopes were covered with firs and larches, their boughs weighed down by snow, and frost-powdered birches and ashes. The ground was covered with the tracks of elk, bears, wolves and many kinds of deer, and here and there we passed the faint imprints of hunters' soft moccasins.

We climbed pass after pass, and the farther we penetrated into the mountains the deeper lay the snow. It grew freezing cold, and one morning, when I crept out of my sleeping-bag, the quicksilver in my thermometer was frozen, and my watch had stopped.

The same afternoon we pitched camp on the line beyond which no trees grew, on the southern slope of a snow-covered pass, and lighted a fire. During the night I was awakened by loud-voiced conversation, and on sticking my head out of the opening of my sleeping-bag, I discovered to my astonishment that we had a guest in the camp. My two travelling companions sat so near the fire that its sparks flew round them, in eager conversation with a thin little hunter. It was clear that what the hunter said was making a profound impression on the two young Buriats, and when I heard the words " Holy Fire Maiden " whispered by the old hunter, I pricked up my ears and crept forward to join them without being noticed.

On my travels down in the steppe country I had often heard obscure references to the " Holy Fire Maiden ", and I had grasped enough to guess that this mysterious being was an all-powerful divinity, and that all the little fire-gods, who watch over the fires in the Mongolian tent hearths, were her vassals. Only once had an old Mongolian friend let a few words drop which conveyed to me that the mysterious being lived among the mountains in a land of snow and ice, whence she ruled over all the little family gods of the Mongolian hearths and over the nomads' destinies. Now I was among mountains in a land of snow and ice. Was I really in the Fire Maiden's country, and should I myself perhaps see this enigmatic being?

All the rest of the night I sat listening breathlessly to the hunter as he told the news from the mountains, and when the new day dawned with sunbeams on snow-powdered mountain sides and glacier peaks gleaming like crystal, I had a feeling that before long I should be standing before the holy altar of the maiden herself.

The reincarnation on earth of the Fire Maiden had been buried under an avalanche four months earlier, and in the time that had passed since this disaster search had been made for the young girl in whom the divine spirit of the dead maiden had taken up its dwelling. Three possible candidates for the honour had been found, and at the impending fire festival it would be revealed which of the three was the new reincarnation of the divinity on earth.

I looked in my diary and saw that we were only six days from the winter solstice; in six days' time it would be the festival of light at home in Christendom, and the festival of fire in this heathen land, tens of thousands of miles from Denmark.

After crossing the pass we descended again through firs and larches laden with snow and frost-powdered birches and ashes; the snow was again covered with tracks of elk, musk-deer, bears and wolves; and then we came upon the first human habitations.

THE HOLY FIRE MAIDEN

Demchik's camp consisted of five smart tents, pitched under cover on the edge of a wood with a view over a wide plateau which in summer must be a marvel of luxuriance. We were delighted to see each other again, and old Demchik sat up late that night reviving our memories from the days when we rode in the same caravan.

I was suddenly roused from my dreams by Demchik, who told me to put on my furs. I went out of the tent with the other men; we got into two waiting sleighs and shot out into the freezing winter night.

The sky was thickly covered with glittering stars, and the snow-clad mountains which framed the steppe shone blue in the light of the rising moon. We swung off to the right into a narrow valley and ascended slowly towards an ice-covered mountain ridge which rose high above the surrounding landscape. We overtook and were overtaken by other sleighs with fur-clad men in them, and when at last we reached the point where the trees stopped, we halted at a place where fifty other sleighs had halted.

Some of the hunters lit torches of rolled-up birch bark, and we all set off towards the high mountain ridge, whence the flames from a huge fire were rising high into the night sky. We came out of the thick snow and made our way cautiously out on to the shining glacier itself. Here the hunters formed up in a semi-circle round the fire.

On the other side of the fire a number of fir trunks stripped of their bark were stacked together to form a tent-like pyramid, with its entrance facing the fire. The trunks were hung about with bones and coloured ribbons, which rattled and fluttered in the faint night breeze. The master of the ceremonies went into the pyramid and flung himself down with his forehead against the ice before a wooden figure carved in a primitive fashion, at whose feet Chinese and Russian coins, compressed tea, tobacco and a great variety of other sacrificial offerings lay heaped.

Several men were occupied in forcing four long poles down into the ice. These poles were hung with strips of cloth in the colours of the dawn, the midday sun, twilight and night, and were fastened to one another by a red string, forming a square round the fire.

The master of the ceremonies stepped out of the pyramid and advanced to the fire ; he was followed by three women

wrapped in big, loose fur coats. Two of them looked scared ; they had to be led to the fire, and their frightened eyes flickered in mute appeal round the circle of silent men. But the third strode forward boldly in front of the master of the ceremonies. She went right up to the fire, whose sparks danced round her ; her white teeth were bared in a voluptuous smile, and her fanatical eyes sought the men's faces with self-assurance.

The master of the ceremonies had been standing with his eyes turned to the flames, whilst he mumbled a string of prayers. Now he suddenly turned towards the three women. The first two shrank back timidly and wrapped themselves more closely in their furs, but the third looked about her proudly and fearlessly.

THE HOLY FIRE MAIDEN

At a sign from the master of the ceremonies two hunters leapt forward to each of the women. The first two resisted and screamed with fear as the men tore off their furs, but the third shook the men off and herself let her yellow fur slip to the ground. With a bearing and mien like an empress she stood right on the edge of the fire, with the glow of the flames full on her red-brown skin, shining with sweat.

Through the crackling of the fire the voice of the master of the ceremonies was heard :

Thou fire, who camest to us, when the mountains were but hillocks, when the trees were twigs.
Thou, whose lot is as a mighty empress',
show us the sign. . .

The young woman on the edge of the fire had stepped back a few paces ; for a moment she stood hesitating, then she leapt through the fire with the agility of a wild beast and landed right in the circle of men, who drew back on all sides in reverence and fear. She looked contemptuously at her two competitors, who, after one or two vain attempts to imitate her leap, were rolling in the snow and howling.

She was so near me that I could smell the sweaty smell from her burnt hair, but she herself noticed nothing. She shook herself like a wet dog, and the drops of sweat formed long pale stripes down her smoke-blackened body. Her black locks moved slightly in the heat from the fire, and she stretched her long supple arms towards it, as if to caress its flames ; her face was full of voluptuous pleasure, and her eyes glowed with fanatical ecstasy.

The master of the ceremonies reverently approached the chosen woman to lead her to the tent-like pyramid of tree-trunks, from the interior of which he brought out a lacquered casket. He took out of this casket chains, diadems and all kinds of ornaments—gleaming corals, turquoises, jade—and decked her with these, while the whole party of men threw

THE HOLY FIRE MAIDEN

themselves on the ground in rapture and reverence for the newly-elected reincarnation of the "Holy Fire Maiden". Then a sable-lined gold brocade cloak was laid about her, and all began to move slowly down to the waiting sleighs to conduct her to the remote mountain temple which is the Holy Fire Maiden's earthly dwelling-place.

I remained alone by the remnants of the dying fire to watch the gleam of torches from the procession as it moved off and listen to the sound of the sleigh-bells among the mountains.

When all was quiet again the stars grew pale, and the topmost peaks slowly assumed the bewitching colours of the dawn. As far as I could see, lay a sea of petrified white billows rolling north and south ; as far as my eyes could reach, no higher point was to be seen than the peak which I had ascended. The whiteness and silence that surrounded me were something I had never experienced.

There was still movement in the remnants of the fire ; the morning breeze played with the charred ribbons of the four poles which symbolized day, twilight, night and dawn ; and at the entrance to the pyramid, the highest altar in Central Asia, lay the ragged fur coat which the girl had worn before she was transformed into the "Holy Fire Maiden ".

THE WHITE OLD MAN OF THE STEPPE

THE " White Old Man of the Steppe " is the protector of the Mongolian pastures and herds. It is he who makes the steppe luxuriant and the nomads prosperous. The " White Old Man of the Steppe " is friendly and genial and wishes happiness to prevail in the world he rules—but at the same time he is a pleasure-loving old fellow, easily tempted into gambling and drunkenness.

His favourite boon companion is the " Dragon Prince ", who is lord of life and death over mankind.

In these two mighty beings we meet pre-Buddhist gods from the primitive mythology of the country, who had become so deeply rooted in the nomads' consciousness that when Buddhism was introduced it was found necessary to include them in its pantheon.

Lamaist priests, wearing grotesque masks representing the White Old Man of the Steppe and the Dragon Prince, are among the group of weird figures which perform the devil dance at the greatest Buddhist temple festival of the year. But besides this a special festival is held in the fifth month of every year—a festival which is entirely the nomads' own and has a far more powerful attraction for them than any of the other temple ceremonies. The meeting-place for this festival, the great summer festival of the steppe, is always one of the *obos* of the tribe. To be present at it is to enter the life of an age long past.

These *obos*, which are usually placed on conspicuous points in the countryside, consist of stones, branches of trees and remains of skeletons, piled up anyhow, but together forming a pyramid whose height and breadth depend on the *obo's* age. They are believed to be resorts of the White Old Man and the Dragon Prince on their visits to earth, and of all the various local spirits in the territory dominated by the *obo*. Many of these *obos* rest on primitive stone foundations, laid centuries ago by a nomad people quite different from that which now lives in the region, and the worship of which they are the object has its roots in the primæval inhabitants of the steppe. They stand like monuments over the steppe, always growing—for no passer-by wants to lose the prosperous journey which he will have if he puts a new stone on the top of the *obo*.

In the spring of 1936 an appeal for help was sent from Inner Mongolia to those nations with whose representatives the suffering tribes had had any contact that inspired confidence. The cause of their hardships was the cattle plague which was devastating the herds of Southern Mongolia, and the specially disastrous consequences of the plague were due to the fact that the herds attacked had just been through the most severe winter in the memory of man. A situation arose on the steppe in which the population was suffering from famine, and the Mongol tribes which had preserved their old culture and way of life were threatened with dissolution and annihilation.

The appeal for help was sent by Teh Wang, the principal

chief of Inner Mongolia, who had always been on friendly terms with foreign explorers visiting his dominions. As the majority of these had been Scandinavians, this appeal was specially addressed to the northern countries.

The distress in the distant nomad country, and the measures for its relief, aroused much greater sympathy in Scandinavia than was to have been expected, and it soon became possible to give help. Dr Joel Eriksson, from the Swedish Mongolia Mission, and Duke Larson, so well known on the steppe, rapidly organized relief for the Chahar and Sunit tribes, and I myself had the opportunity of collaborating with Georg Söderbom among the Tumet and Darkhan Beil tribes, lying farther to the west. The difficulties were great and of many kinds ; but they could all be surmounted, and I have never undertaken a more interesting and rewarding task. It was a long struggle against firmly implanted traditions and primitive superstition—we did not wish to destroy these, but it was necessary to tone them down ; an adventurous campaign, in which it was our difficult task to convert our natural opponents into enthusiastic champions and to make the most fatalistic people in the world offer confident resistance to the will of hidden natural forces. But the work was inspiring and rich in unforeseen reward.

The situation was in fact this. If we could not enable the distressed tribes to continue their nomad existence, and give them courage to take up their life anew, the vast areas of Mongolia, which can only support a nomad population, would be depopulated, and the last of the inhabitants who still preserved the old steppe traditions, and whose chiefs were descendants of the Great Mongol Jenghiz Khan himself, would be compelled to flee southward, to the swarming lowlands of China. Here they would quickly be transformed into a miserable, mendicant scum among the trading people over whom so many of their earlier generations had ruled.

The distribution of the foodstuffs we had brought from the coast in the form of flour and groats, and our plans for supplying the completely empty camps with new cattle, were received by the population with both pleasure and gratitude. But as soon as we attempted to inoculate the animals which were still not infected, and to burn the thousands of carcasses which lay strewn over the steppe, we encountered the most violent resistance, which threatened to bring us into collision with all the high priests and magicians who represented the mighty occult powers of the wild. We were completely powerless in face of this opposition so long as we did not understand the fundamental cause of it ; and we were, therefore, always on the look-out for every detail which could throw light upon the nomads' strictly guarded secrets.

Our watchfulness was rewarded, and little by little, as our insight grew deeper, we became able to arrange our plan of work in a manner which gradually gained us the confidence of even our most bitter opponents. From that moment the imminent danger, which had threatened the Mongols' continued existence as a free nomad people, was averted.

We had all the cattle we took with us inoculated before they could cross the pass on to the Mongolian high plateau, where we let them mix at once with the worst infected herds instead of first distributing them to the future owners. The fact that none of our inoculated beasts were attacked by the plague—indeed, sometimes one of them was the only survivor of a whole herd, the rest being exterminated despite all the lamas' prayers and spells—made a deep impression on the unhappy population. The influential priests and magicians, however, still disapproved of our foreign methods, and it was only when we had discovered the real cause of their opposition that we were able to lay a foundation of confidence based on which our own imagination could continue the good work. Every new detail which was brought to our knowledge inspired us to the narration of highly-coloured stories such as the inhabitants of the steppe had never heard of, and which we could never have invented in any other milieu.

The most important cause of the nomads' objection to our

attempts to limit and fight the cattle plague was their reluctance to encroach on the rights of others. For all the steppe cattle, on which the nomads' existence depended, were owned by the White Old Man of the Steppe, who generously allowed the Mongols to administer and exploit his wealth.

But the White Old Man of the Steppe was weak in face of many temptations. He often gambled with the Dragon Prince, the ruler of all human sicknesses and lord of life and death, and as the two mighty beings had to pay in their currencies, the poor Mongols always had to suffer for it. If the Dragon Prince lost, he demanded the requisite number of human lives, and if the White Old Man was unlucky, he had to spread cattle plague among his herds to obtain the necessary means of payment. If we tried to deprive the White Old Man of his rights over the life and death of his cattle, then, it was feared, one or other of the two powerful gamblers would fly into a furious rage which could have even more disastrous consequences for the Mongols.

We identified the White Old Man of the Steppe with the St Nicholas of the Russian Church, whom we enrolled in the Scandinavian pantheon. White-bearded Nicholas became the great reformer of Scandinavian cattle-breeding; thanks to him a Northern cow had at least one calf a year, and every one of our cows gave as much milk as ten Mongolian cows, in addition to cheese, which gave manliness, youthfulness and strength. We translated and declaimed the turgid advertising blurbs on our American canned meat tins, and attributed them all to the dairy products of our own country. And all this, we declared, had come about because old Nicholas had taught us to collect hay in stacks against severe winters and to inoculate our cattle against the deadly cattle plague.

Thanks to our willingness to learn, both we and old Nicholas had become so inordinately prosperous that he could gamble as much as he liked without its leading to any catastrophe. This was a thing that interested the Mongols; and we had to invent more stories about St Nicholas. We turned all the agricultural schools in Scandinavia into sort of *obo* temples on a grand scale, where tens of thousands of priests and disciples conducted services and made offerings to the glory of St Nicholas. St John's Eve became the yearly *obo* festival, at which sacred fires were lighted in honour of the cattle and dragon princes, and we brought in the Olympic Games, with their many sporting contests in the presence of great chiefs, as a part of the same festival. The Mongols listened tensely and reverently, and gradually they became the most eager champions of the view that old Nicholas must be a sort of divine twin brother of the White Old Man of the Steppe, and that the two philanthropic but frivolous ancients were two differently acclimatized reincarnations of the same original divinity. We equipped old Nicholas with virtues and vices similar to those which the Mongols attributed to their White Old Man. We made him genial and pleasure-loving, and in honour of him and his steppe-born twin brother we got on our wireless sets all the cheerful lively music available on the air.

At last the situation turned in our favour to such a degree that even the most ill-disposed magicians and enemies of everything modern gave us both their blessing and their support, so that they too might share in and contribute to the impending salvation of which no one any longer doubted.

In the course of May all the cattle which had not been attacked were inoculated, and at the end of the month the epidemic was over and a third of the cattle of the two tribes was saved. But in spite of the growing spring grass the steppe was still an awful sight. Thousands and thousands of dead beasts lay strewn over it, and we had to invent and tell new stories before we could get the Mongols to collect the carcasses and pile them on to giant pyres, thus depriving the predatory beasts and birds of the steppe of their rightful booty.

So passed the Mongols' fifth month, and a delicate veil of blossoms spread over the green luxuriant steppe. The plague was stamped out ; all the visible devastation had disappeared ;

the herds, ravaged by winter and sickness, became once more fat and healthy and promised to multiply. We had distributed the cattle, which we had collected for the impoverished camps, in such a way that every camp would own at least one cow with calf plus ten sheep ; this could be regarded as sufficient to keep starvation away from the tents until the new stock had multiplied and fair-sized herds and sources of income had been formed.

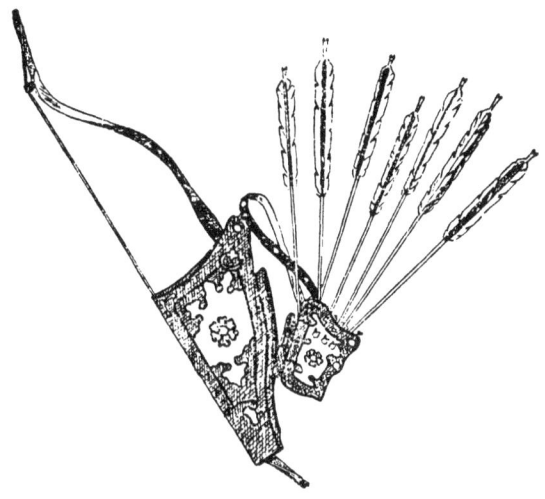

And now it was time to think about the great *obo* festival, which this year was to be especially grand—partly to thank the White Old Man of the Steppe for having spared enough cattle for the Mongols to continue their nomad existence, and partly to give the pleasure-loving old fellow a tremendous feast, which should keep him for a long time from further excesses, so disastrous for the Mongols.

The astrologers of the tribe had calculated what would be the luckiest day for the festival ; it was to be held at Altan *obo*, the " Golden *Obo* ". The most splendid ceremonial robes were unpacked from the bottom of chests ; men worked feverishly at saddle-cloths and the embroidery on the new riding boots ; and the many heavy silver ornaments were cleaned and polished till they shone like the sun.

On the eve of the festival Söderbom and I reached a camp a few miles from the Golden *Obo*. In all the tents of the camp we found a number of horsemen from more out-of-the-way districts, all wanting to be sure of missing nothing of the next day's ceremonies. They were all wearing their finest clothes, and all looked forward to the day with the enthusiastic anticipation of children. Often a tent would suddenly fall silent without any reason that I could understand, and the men turned towards the door listening, or peered through the open smoke-vent, with the expression of children who imagine they hear Father Christmas's footsteps. Newly arrived horsemen told in whispers of the experiences they had had on their way. There were stories of invisible hands feeling their beasts' manes and tails ; of hoofmarks which appeared and disappeared after invisible cavalcades had galloped past ; of sand and dust which in mysterious fashion were blown right against the wind ; and of much else which on any other night of the year would have stupefied the nomads. Now all these alleged experiences and imagined signs only pleased them, for they proved that the Dragon Prince with his merry retinue had descended the arch of the rainbow to their steppe to be present at the impending *obo* festival.

In the tents of the camp we found the best marksmen of the different clans with their heaviest bows and longest arrows ; wrestlers, polishing the copper-work on their armour-like leather waistcoats ; and mothers putting the last touch to the embroidered dresses which their sons would wear in the great race.

At last the dawn came—a morning worthy of the festal day, one of those fresh green midsummer mornings on which one forgets that there can be suffering and poverty on the steppe as well—on which one wakes, wide awake at once, to the sound of the thundering hoofbeats of unruly herds of cattle, to the resonant neighing of half-wild horses, and dashes out of the tent, full of life, in order to miss none of the new day's enjoyments. Outside the tent the whole steppe was strewn with the dewdrops of the night, sparkling like fairy gems among flowers and leaves in the soft light of the dawn.

And yonder, over the green shoulder of the hill, rose the imposing pinnacle of the Golden *Obo*. At its foot a number of red-robed priests were busy laying the sacrificial fires, and a gaily clad party of shepherds were putting up tents and awnings for their distinguished masters.

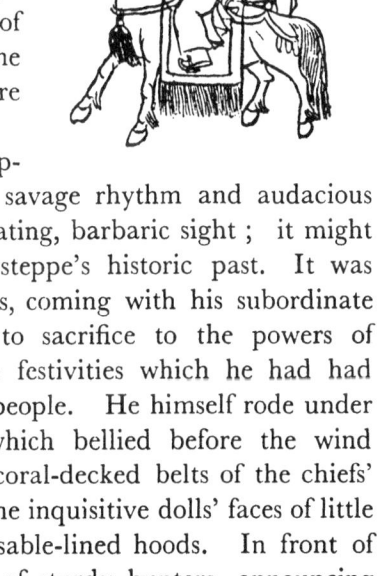

When the sun rose above the heights to eastwards, the steppe was already full of parties of galloping horsemen ; they came from all quarters and all were making for the Golden *Obo*.

Suddenly there came a galloping cavalcade which with its savage rhythm and audacious display of colours was a fascinating, barbaric sight ; it might have been a vision from the steppe's historic past. It was Sha-Beis, chief of those steppes, coming with his subordinate chiefs and his large retinue to sacrifice to the powers of the *obo* and take part in the festivities which he had had prepared for himself and his people. He himself rode under a canopy in five colours, which bellied before the wind like a sail in a storm. The coral-decked belts of the chiefs' wives rattled with silver, and the inquisitive dolls' faces of little princesses peered from under sable-lined hoods. In front of the cavalcade rode a couple of sturdy hunters, announcing their highnesses' arrival with loud cracking of long-lashed whips, and weather-beaten men-at-arms, whose feathered arrows stood out like spread eagles' wings from the quivers fastened on their backs, brought up the rear.

A party of priests approached from another direction, their golden-yellow robes and lacquered hats gleaming in the sunshine. The priests rode at a dignified trot, escorting a carriage in their midst under whose blue roof Delevar Gegen himself, the " living Buddha " from Khalkha, sat in a meditative Buddha posture.

Both parties made for the blue awning on the southern slope of the hill, where Sha-Beis and Delevar Gegen and their chief men were invited to occupy the seats of honour.

The fire which had been laid round the *obo* was lighted, and sepia columns of smoke rose straight towards the blue sky. All those taking part in the festival stood in a wide semi-circle

facing the blue canopy; their number, approaching a thousand, made an overpowering impression out on the steppe, where one is accustomed to regard a dozen people as a crowd. The "living Buddha" rose from his yellow seat of honour and, followed by a group of high priests, strode up to a long sacrificial table which had been placed near the southernmost fire.

From the top of the *obo* two red-robed lamas blew long blasts on their conches across the steppe; other lamas poured melted butter on the sacrificial fires; and as the flames flickered up towards the sky the "living Buddha" called on the heavenly powers and invited them to come and be present.

Conqueror ! thou who in all eternity hast had compassion on the sinner ;
Thou, subduer of all passions, who hast kept thy oath,
Oh show us, when thy time comes, from pure spheres, thy wonders !
Come with thy pure hosts and help us and preserve us.

A party of shepherds came dragging five newly-slaughtered sheep and cut them up with practised hands. The best pieces of fat and meat were then laid on the sacrificial table, after which they were flung on to the *obo*, on to the sacrificial fire and high into the air, amid the strained attention of all the spectators. To the evident joy of all, the offerings were well received by the heavenly powers, for the pieces of meat

thrown high into the air were seized by circling birds of prey, and the smoke from the fires rose into the sky like white pillars.

This ascertained, the festival now took its cheerful course without restraint. Wrestlers met in strenuous duels, till the tribe's best man could be chosen ; the archers' arrows whistled towards the targets ; and then the crowd collected to watch its favourite spectacle—a race between the youngest men of the tribe on their most famous horses. After the race the winning horses were led up to Sha-Beis and they and their riders decorated with sky-blue scarves, while one of the tribe's old masters of the ceremonies paid to the horse the traditional verbal tribute which, from the beginning of time, the best horses on the steppe have received. Amulets of the " living Buddha " are hung about the winning horses' necks ; they are let loose on the steppe and thereafter only used for sport.

Afterwards the participators assembled round the *obo* fire to consume the offerings of food which were left over, or scattered in groups round the other fires on the steppe to discuss the pleasures of the day and the bright prospects for the future. Long after sunset and on till the new dawn the old steppe songs were sung and wine-cups raised towards the glittering stars, till all sombre memories were wiped out and the tribe looked to the future with cheerful confidence.

TO A WEDDING FEAST AMONG THE CHAHAR PEOPLE

ONE day in February I received a formal invitation to be present at the *hurum*, or wedding feast, at which Bato-Merin's high-spirited son was to carry off Naidung Taichi's bashful little daughter. Bato-Merin, the bridegroom's father, had invited me, and I started for the feast very early, as etiquette required that I should be among those who sent the chief's son off on his wooing expedition, with which the feast begins.

It was − 30 degrees Celsius[1] when I crept out of my sleeping-bag. Out in the clear frosty winter night stood my two Mongol companions, warming the horses' bits in the dying embers of the night fire. We straddled over the embers in turn to warm up everything inside the long fur coats before we sprang into the icy cold saddles. Then we surrendered ourselves to the marvel that awaited us—to the joy of

[1] − 22 deg. Fahrenheit.

galloping over crackling snow under glittering stars to a new experience.

We overtook and were overtaken by other parties of horsemen bound for the same destination, and as the number of horses grew their fire and pace increased; for horses, like many humans, love to gallop in company. All the horsemen were in their grandest attire; their silver ornaments jingled as they rode, and the women's ruddy faces looked out smiling from their coiffures framed with coral and turquoises.

Our cavalcade swung into the canyon which concealed Bato-Merin's winter camp, and the brilliant colours of the approaching sunrise spread like floating gold over the snow of the mountain crests.

About fifty yards from the camp to the south-west a row of tall stakes was stuck into the ground, and a long leather rope was stretched between them. We tethered our steaming horses to this, tidied ourselves up a little and took our places at the back with old Bimba Noyen. Apart from his hereditary rank, he had the honour of being *tengerin moriksang avo*—" heaven-worshipping father "—at this feast; he was to act as a sort of master of the ceremonies and see that the feast went off smoothly without a single one of the profoundly significant rites being omitted.

Bimba Noyen and all the guests set off at a dignified, swinging pace which set the long brocade robes, the long hanging knives and the many heavy silver ornaments rattling and glittering as they swung to and fro.

A low altar had been set up south of the camp. It was piled to overflowing with the traditional offerings of meat, milk and wine, and behind—facing the guests—stood Bato-Merin and his nearest relations.

The two groups greeted one another with dignity, sinking slowly down on to the right knee and touching the snow-covered steppe with the right hand.

Then the young bridegroom came forward. He was accompanied by his older and younger foster-brothers and the four brideswomen, chosen from among the youngest of those women at whose weddings Bato-Merin himself had acted as " heaven-worshipping father ". Two of the women carried

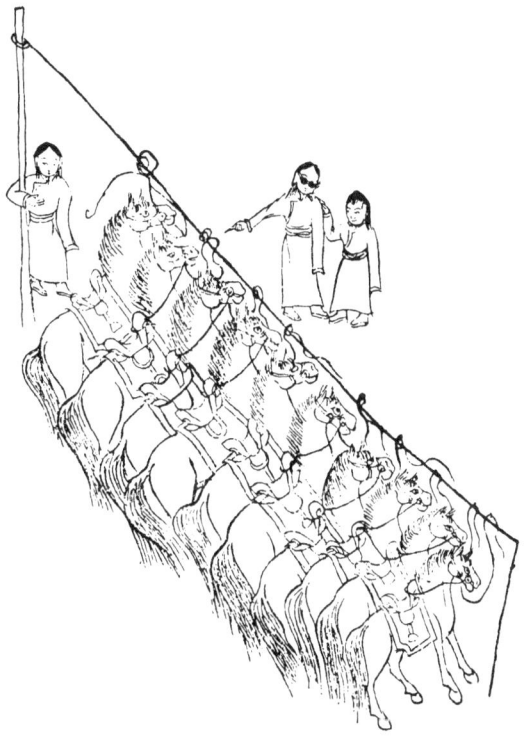

old weapons of the tribe, which they fastened to the bridegroom's slender waist, and the two others greased the weapons with fat and splashed them with wine from the sacrificial table. The " heaven-worshipping father " took a silver-mounted cup full of milk and flung its contents to the four quarters of the globe, pronouncing as he did so the *bellig uge*, an ancient piece of ritual which the moment demanded.

The bridegroom's attendants led him to the waiting horses, and as he got into the saddle a smoking stick of incense was carried round him three times. Then he galloped off over the steppe, accompanied by the " heaven-worshipping father ", his foster-brothers, and the dozen men who were his youngest and best friends.

In Bato-Merin's camp the hours that followed were spent in preparations for the reception of the bride. White columns of smoke rose from the vents of the six tents, and there was a smell of hot food.

A look-out man shouted that the bridegroom and his escort were in sight, and all except the cooks streamed out to the post to which the horses were tethered. Shouts and yells were heard from the steppe, and a moment later the advance-guard of the bridal party swung into Bato-Merin's valley and rode at a furious gallop towards the blue cloth fluttering on a tall mast and indicating the " lucky quarter " from which the bride was to enter the camp that was to be her future home.

The young bridegroom sat tall and straight in his new saddle, his young face and bright eyes full of the ecstasy of his accomplished wooing. One leap and he stood on the ground, victoriously contemplating the smoke from the bridal tent.

TO A WEDDING FEAST AMONG THE CHAHAR PEOPLE

The brideswomen hurried up and took from him his bow, quiver and sword, which they laid on the roof of the marriage tent as a sign that none might enter it.

Inside the covered wagon bumping and jolting across the steppe, the bride lay sobbing, her face buried in her mother's lap ; but the sounds of her grief were silenced by the horses'

hoof-beats and the cries and shouts of joy of the surrounding horsemen.

The cavalcade came to a sudden halt at the post, and both bride and bridegroom, with their escorts, advanced to the sacrificial table south of the camp. The bridegroom fell on his knees and nine times bent over and touched the steppe with his forehead, while the " heaven-worshipping father " called down the blessings of heaven and of the two clans' ancestors on the impending union.

Then the bride was led by her relations and the rest of her suite to the tent of her father- and mother-in-law to ask permission to enter Bato-Merin's clan ; but they were stopped in front of the entrance by one of Bato-Merin's sons, who required of them the information and guarantees that tradition demanded. When these formalities had been satisfactorily carried out, and the veiled bride had made her curtsey to Bato-Merin and his wife, the bridegroom's women of honour led her to the bridal tent, outside which all the guests had collected to watch with curiosity the handing over of her dowry.

There were long chalk-white under-boots, small embroidered riding-boots, hats with fringes and tassels, dresses and cloaks for festal occasions and for work—all, in fact, that a chief's young wife desires and needs. The number of everything was a multiple of the mystic figure nine; and the grand total of each item was called out by the person handing it over and repeated in a loud voice by the women of honour inside the tent. They were busily occupied in packing away the dowry into the new chests in the bridal tent.

Then the party went out of the camp to count and take stock of the camp's new herds of horses, flocks of sheep, and other beasts, which also were in multiples of nine.

And while the young bride sat weeping in the new tent, where the women of honour were loosening her maiden plaits and putting up her hair into the coiffure, decked with coral and heavy with silver, which distinguishes the chiefs' wives of the clan, the bridegroom was sitting impatiently in another tent, to which only he and his two foster-brothers had access.

All the wedding-guests streamed into the two guest tents, where Bato-Merin and his wife presided, and took their places according to rank. In the men's tent the " heaven-worshipping father " sat in the northern seat of honour, and to him Bato-Merin handed the first of the large cups of wine. As he received it he paid tribute to the wine, as was meet on such a festal day. While he praised the wine, he splashed it on to the flames of the fire, the tent altar and the smoke-vent, and then drained the cup to the dregs.

Bato-Merin refilled the cup to offer it to the guest next in importance, and so continued till all the guests were sitting licking their lips for more. Then the " heaven-worshipping father " took the brimming cup and handed it to Bato-Merin, while all the guests rose on the left knee and with uplifted palms invited the host to taste the wine himself. This concluded the first round.

The wine-drinking went on with large cups, round after round, till the smell of food from the kitchen tent grew unendurable. Then large dishes, but small cups of wine, were set before the guests.

All now disposed themselves in quite a new manner. The long sleeves were tucked up above the elbows, the sharp knives drawn from their silver-mounted sheaths, and the eyes of all were turned to the tent door. This was drawn aside, and a string of young men glided in behind steaming savoury-smelling dishes. These were placed before the " heaven-worshipping father ". Piles of meat lay on the dishes ; the unflayed legs and the twitching fat tails hung over the edges, and on the top of each dish lay the slaughtered beasts' unflayed heads, with eyes staring and tongues hanging out.

When all the dishes stood in a row before the master of the ceremonies, he cut a cross in the forehead of each sheep's head ; then he cut off the choice bits from the fat tails, threw part on the fire and laid part on the altar table. With practised hand he cut the masses of meat into generous portions, which were quickly handed round to the guests according to their rank and importance. Then the guests abandoned themselves to unrestrained gorging, as only those can who have often suffered from unstilled hunger. But weeks of hunger and privation can be made up for in half an hour, and the diners soon sought a new enjoyment. They loosed the long sashes which at first had pressed so tight round their slim waists, unbuttoned their high collars, and disposed themselves in comfortable attitudes.

A few cups of wine are enough for a man ; and in order to

turn those few into many, stimulating songs and games were invented generations ago. All these songs have this in common, that certain verses are accompanied by one or more finger signs, which mean that each finger catches or is caught by another. The simplest of these games is one in which one can show with one's fingers " stone, sack or scissors ". Stone is caught in sack ; scissors cut holes in sack ; but stone resists scissors.

Gradually a desire for song and music crept over the company, and the steppe troubadours, whose calling and task it is to interpret the old-time musical traditions to new generations, assembled. They glided into the tent and took their places inside the entrance on the southern edge of the fire ; there was the man with the " four-eared violin " and the man with the " horse's head violin ", the man with the " stick whose sound is like the wind in the rushes ", and another with a banjo-like instrument. They tightened their strings and sang of horses, war and love, while the guests groaned and grunted with repletion.

While all this is going on in the guests' tent, the unhappy bride is undressed by the bridegroom's women of honour and laid among pillows behind the curtain which conceals the north side of the tent. Then the fire in the bridal tent is put out, and the bride's four women of honour lead the bridegroom into its darkness ; there he is undressed and made to lie down byt he side of the girl, whose face he may never have seen.

The eight women sit up all night in the tent on the other side of the curtain which hides the newly-married pair—four to protect the bride's rights, four the bridegroom's.

An atmosphere of melancholy had spread through the two guest tents. The men called their women, the women crept up to their husbands ; and they dreamed of the time when they themselves slept in a tent whose roof was decorated with the clan's weapons.

Eredin Monke's camp lay some miles from the wedding camp, and I and my escort managed to get there fairly early. When the new day dawned, I was therefore able to observe its events with a clearer eye than the other participators.

When I got back to the wedding camp at sunrise, a new orgy of eating and drinking was going on, and I have seldom seen people with a worse "hangover" than that morning. But although so much the worse for wear, they were all cordial to a pale foreigner like myself, and when the principal ceremony of the feast was due to begin, I was compelled to take the best place in the bridal tent after the place of honour which the " heaven-worshipping father " occupied. This dignitary was a much sought after guest. He was no longer young, his eyes were bloodshot, and he had difficulty in sitting up straight in his seat of honour. All the most important wedding guests had been summoned to the impending ceremony, the *clou* of the day. Most of them were infirm and found it hard to live up to their reputation of old times.

The young couple were brought in. The bridegroom took up his position south of the fire facing the " heaven-worshipping father ", and the bride inside the eastern pole of the tent entrance. Her head was bowed in humility, but she was no longer weeping, and her shining head ornaments jingled every time she glanced at her young lord.

All except the bridal pair tried to eat a little of the dainties which were served, and at last the whole of the bride's retinue rose to set out on their journey homeward. The bride no longer paid any attention to them, and when, in accordance with tradition, three of her kinsmen came back a few minutes

later to offer her the chance of accompanying them to the home camp, she shook her head vigorously.

The tent was emptied of the last of her kinsmen, and of the guests who remained the majority were now sleeping peacefully. Dull eyes were turned towards the " heaven-worshipping father " and the ancient ceremonial sword which stood leaning against him. But the old dignitary was fast asleep with his head resting heavily on my shoulder. A dreamlike silence prevailed in the tent ; only the bride and bridegroom quivered with impatient expectancy. The bride's veiled face was turned towards the old sword in the lap of the " heaven-worshipping father ", and the bridegroom had turned towards the veiled face.

TO A WEDDING FEAST AMONG THE CHAHAR PEOPLE

I looked at the young bridegroom, the fuddled guests in the tent, and then at the young bride—her little embroidered boots, her delicate form and her veiled face. And I was infected by the bridegroom's impatience ; what was hidden behind the blue veil ?

" *Ili jaboho dalde jaboho,*" I whispered to her, and " *Ili jabo,*" both bride and bridegroom whispered eagerly in reply.

So I seized the ceremonial sword and with its point slowly and reverently lifted the blue veil from the bride's face and commanded her and her husband to live under the same tent-roof. She cannot have been more than fifteen, and her face was pretty and full of zest for life.

In the days and weeks that followed I listened to many accounts of the wedding in Bato-Merin's camp. It had been a fine wedding, at which fourteen beakers and twenty-eight cups of wine had been drunk, corresponding to seven pints —50 per cent. alcohol—per head.

I noticed that quite a new interest was being shown in my son's age, and an anxiety to calculate when he would be marriageable. I obtained an explanation of this curiosity when I heard that the young bride, whose veil I had thrown off in Bato-Merin's camp, was now bound to act as woman of honour on the day when my son should be dressed in his wedding garments and girt with arms to carry off his chosen wife.

I have talked it over with my boy, and the idea appeals to him enormously.

But I am afraid that before that time comes the last *tengerein moriksang avo* will have ascended to his heavens, and that the nomads will have learned other customs than those they have inherited from their remote ancestors.

A NOMAD'S FUNERAL

TSARAN GERIL, an old Mongol caravan leader, and I had once been travelling companions on a long journey. Despite the great difference between us in age and colour, religion and knowledge, we had come to understand and respect each other's view of life.

A NOMAD'S FUNERAL

When I set out on my first independent journey, I was full of pride in the size and modern equipment of my caravan and full of exhortations to the man to whom I had entrusted its leadership. But before the journey was over, I was listening to the old man as to the wise counsel of a father, and I loved his talk, which gave me knowledge that my ancestors had lost generations before.

On our marches through steppes, deserts and mountains I had but seldom an opportunity of exchanging words and opinions with old Tsaran Geril, for he was either occupied with the many important duties of a caravan leader, or riding alone, deep in thought or dreams which I did not venture to disturb.

I still see vividly the sight which I then enjoyed so often—his slender figure giving supplely to his camel's rocking motion, an indescribable peace upon his weather-beaten, time-worn features, and his hawk's eyes, at other times so sharp, fixed dreamily on the far horizon for which we were making. Day after day, month after month, we journeyed through the same grand scenery, shared the same experiences and heard the same sounds ; and perhaps it was all these common impressions which made us mutually receptive and brought about our friendship.

When the evening camp fires were shooting up towards the stars of the night sky, and the grazing camels loomed up like phantom beasts against the background of steppe, he used to impart his wisdom to me.

There was not much we did not discuss in these nocturnal conversations, and there was a great deal in what he told me against which my sober understanding rebelled. But we were far away from the milieu in which I had imbibed my western knowledge, and all the impressions of the day, the mysterious pulse-beats of the wild, were in alliance with Tsaran Geril's convinced view of life. When the fed camels grunted in their sleep, the White Old Man, lord of all cattle, glided over the prairie to count his riches ; the Dragon Prince sped through

A NOMAD'S FUNERAL

the mountain passes with the sigh of the wind to receive the sacrifices laid on the stone altars of the *obos* ; and the dreaded Erlik Khan, ruler of the kingdom of death, flung up with his powerful horns the sandstorms which draw men into his kingdom.

The journey I made in Tsaran Geril's company was one of his last. He afterwards pitched his camp near the starting-point of the great caravan routes at Kalgan, so that the camel-bells could always inspire his dreams and he could discuss the news from distant parts with the younger caravan men who were now treading in his footsteps.

Here, in his last camp, in the years that followed, I often visited him and his family on my journey to and from many destinations in Mongolia. The last time I visited him he was ill and worn out, and fearlessly declared that he would soon follow Erlik Khan.

When I had done eight days' marches northward from his camp, I was overtaken by a horseman who begged me to turn back to the camp. My friend, he said, was on the point of death ; the lamas had declared that his illness was neither one of the hundred and one afflictions which could be cured with medicine nor one of the hundred and one pains which could be removed by prayers and sacrifices, but was one of the hundred and one sicknesses which broke the tent-poles of life itself.

A long way from the camp we rode past its many dogs, already tied up, sniffing and growling in the direction of the camp. " Tsaran Geril is dead," my guide said, " and the dogs have been tied up to prevent them from falling upon the body till the right time comes."

We checked our gallop and rode at a foot's pace towards the light columns of smoke which flickered up on the night wind, like funeral banners, from the roof openings of the tents. We rode to the horses' tethering place and dismounted. The stillness of the grave hung over the camp ; the dogs had gone, the folds were empty, and no one came to meet us with a cheerful greeting. I looked towards the tent, at whose fire I had spent so many hours in Tsaran Geril's company, and I was filled with grief at the thought that I should never again listen to his poetical talk or glimpse the dreams of the nomad soul in his deep firm eyes.

Suddenly a sound was heard from Tsaran Geril's tent; it sounded like the sigh of a passing soul, rising from the steppe to seek out all the mysterious powers which hold sway over it. The voice rose and fell, continued steadily for a time and suddenly changed to a hectic, breathless tempo, as if it came from a spirit in flight. Long-drawn mournful flutings broke the stream of monotonous formulas, and muffled drum-beats sounded like an enchantment from another world.

It was the lamas repeating the magic formulas of the *paddum* for the dead man's soul. They were praying that the spirit Tut might quickly free itself from the body; praying to exorcise the spirit Schiolma, who would otherwise cling fast to the earthly remains " until sand disappears from the earth ", and to drive away the spirit Dzitker, who would take up his abode with those whom the dead man left behind, spreading death and disaster by his very presence.

I saw my companion from the camp looking about him nervously and listening tensely for sounds from the steppe, while he ran his rosary quickly through his fingers; he was listening for the invisible spirits of death, watching for Schiolma's ten-headed form hovering noiselessly in the air and for Erlik Khan himself in his incarnation as a blue stag.

We crept into the death tent, into the flickering light of the butter lamps and the fire, into the atmosphere full of the sweet smell of incense, into the noise of the exorcising lamas.

To the left of the fire, with his back to the west side of the tent, sat the *haikh-Lama*, learned in astrology. He wore a tall orange felt hat, shaped like a Roman gladiator's helmet. Long black silk fringes hung down from it, and over his yellow silk robe he wore a broad gaily-coloured collar of stiff brocade. He sat with crossed legs on a yellow silk cushion ; before him, on a low sacrificial table, lay all the magic books and ritual objects required for the ceremony. He mumbled and intoned so eagerly and vigorously that his hot breath set the silk fringes which hung down before his face in violent motion.

At certain passages in the service he stretched out his bare arms to grasp in his supple fingers the objects which the coming ceremony required. Now it was the yellowed thighbone of an innocent girl who had died in her eighteenth year ; next time, a drum shaped like an hour-glass and made from the skulls of two simple but good men ; next time a pair of cymbals, whose sound was pleasing to the gods, and whose long ringing note told the initiated that their metal contained the prescribed quantity of salt from the sacred mines in Tibet.

A NOMAD'S FUNERAL

On a black silk cloth in the *haikh-Lama's* lap lay thirteen peculiar metal instruments, representing axes, picks, forks and knives of all shapes. When his chanting reached a high pitch of excitement, he juggled menacingly with these implements against a human figure of clay which stood on the sacrificial table.

The *haikh-Lama's* assistant lamas were all dressed in red robes and wore on their heads a sort of five-leaved crown, on the outsides of which Lamaistic images were painted. They carried in a heavy image of gilded bronze and placed it on

the west side of the hearth. It represented the god of death himself, and its hollow interior must have been filled with powdered incense, for after one of the lamas had thrown an ember from the fire into its wide jaws, it spat a pillar of heavy-smelling incense.

Against the east side of the tent sat old Tsaran Geril's widow surrounded by her few relatives. Old Jeshigema had seen her husband set out on many perilous journeys, and she had worked and toiled that on his return he might find an abundant stock of cattle and a secure food supply. Now she was taking leave of him on the longest of all his long journeys—for whom was she now to work, for whom should she store up in chests? There were only five old relatives by her side, for the three

A NOMAD'S FUNERAL

children the gods had given her were all born while Tsaran Geril was away on his long caravan journeys—and they all died before he ever saw them.

She sat among her old relatives, small and shrunken, the glittering silver ornaments in her hair covered with white cloth, her eyes—usually so observant and cheerful—staring in hopeless but dry-eyed despair at a cloth which hung from the roof-beams. One guessed that the old caravan leader's dead body lay behind the cloth.

Now and then old Jeshigema cast a look at the shallow tea-cup on the sacrificial table. Every time steam ceased to rise from it, she got up and replaced the cold drink with boiling tea. I recognized the old smoke-blackened birch-wood cup with its always bright silver mounting: it was Tsaran Geril's tea-cup, from which I had so often seen him drink, and from which he had so often invited me to drink.

The lamas' mumbling voices rose and fell; their monotonous repetition of prayers and formulas was interrupted only when the ritual instruments broke in with single notes or with a diabolical noise to attract or drive away the spirits hovering round. Nothing else happened in the tent; no one said a word, and everyone let his thoughts follow the course which the hour and the ceremony directed.

Suddenly the tent became silent; the *haikh-Lama* had reached the *barede-sildep*, the conclusion of the rite, and, now completely exhausted, collapsed over the sacrificial table. The lamas sighed and breathed heavily; all else in the tent was as deathly still as the steppe outside.

After a time one of them rose with a couple of shining instruments in his hand, and went behind the curtain to the dead man. A few hard blows, which made Jeshigema start, were heard from within. The *haikh-Lama* had risen and was peering at the smoke-vent. Then a hollow sound was heard; the hard blows stopped. The lama had bored through Tsaran Geril's skull with his fine chisel and little brass hammer, that the soul might be able to free itself from the dead body.

A NOMAD'S FUNERAL

A breath of wind from the steppe passed over the camp and made the praying flags hoisted over the tent rustle gently. All glanced uneasily at the tensely listening *haikh-Lama*. Then he looked down again and announced to the anxious Jeshigema that Tsaran Geril's soul was in good company and that the " casting out " of his dead body could take place in three days.

Early on the morning of the third day I rode with the *haikh-Lama* to Bayan Dokhom, one of the " casting-out " places of the Adochen tribe—the place where the dead are laid out to feed the predatory beasts and birds of the steppe. Cicero and other old writers tell us that this kind of funeral is a very ancient custom among the nomads of Asia ; it was already in use, they say, several centuries before our era.

Bayan Dokhom is an area of about two and a half square miles, in the midst of which a small reedy lake collects the water from the neighbouring heights. Seen from the pass which is the natural entrance to the area, the little lake set in a hollow, gleaming blue against the luxuriant green of the surrounding slopes, is idyllically beautiful. But not a tent is to be seen, no cattle wade in the lush grass, and one wonders that there are no camps in the place, nor any sign of life. It was not till the *haikh-Lama* had dismounted and taken out of a skin bag a quantity of dorsal vertebræ, which he began to throw on the ground, that I realized that we had reached our destination.

After each throw the lama closely examined the position of the dorsal vertebræ on the ground, after which he collected them, put them back in his bag, and moved off in a new direction. And now the place began slowly to come to life. Eagles, vultures, and other birds of prey flapped up out of the reeds and the long grass and circled round over our heads with their easy gliding flight ; and large packs of black Mongolian dogs appeared on the crests of the hills. These were the savage marauders of the steppe, scenting the preparations for their feeding-time.

A NOMAD'S FUNERAL

The *haikh-Lama* continued on his zig-zag course across the steppe, seeking his way to his goal. The nearer we came to the bottom of the saucer in the steppe, the more uneasy my horse became. Everywhere bleached skeletons and grinning human skulls lay half-hidden in the long grass, and at places they lay in such masses that I had to get off and lead my terrified horse.

On the other side of the lake, on a western slope which the morning sun had not yet reached, the *haikh-Lama* found the place which had been chosen by the unseen powers to be Tsaran Geril's " casting-out place ", and he immediately set about buying from the " lord of the earth " the right to use the place. First he drew with an antelope's horn a human figure on the earth, and then, a little way north of this drawing, he stuck into the earth an arrow with a many-coloured ribbon attached to it. Then he enclosed the place with five sticks and fastened them together with plaited hairs from a horse's tail. Lastly he covered the human figure he had drawn with a white blanket, and placed two untanned goatskins to south-east and south-west of it.

During all these preparations birds of prey had gathered above our heads in flocks that grew thicker and thicker, and the wild dogs had dared to approach to a distance of a few hundred yards, whence, with tongues hanging out, they attentively watched the course of the preparations.

Soon after these were finished, the funeral procession itself appeared up in the pass. At the head rode Tsaran Geril's brother, leading at his side a saddled but riderless horse. This was Tsaran Geril's favourite horse, and across its saddle lay a red blanket—the same blanket which had adorned the saddle on which Jeshigema rode when she entered her lord's camp as a young bride. Now his released spirit was held to be occupying this honoured position. Tsaran Geril's brother wore on his breast a yellow handkerchief on which a quantity of figures and formulas were painted in black Chinese ink. This was *Baante Hurel*, the magic banner which sweeps away all evil on the funeral procession's route. Behind Tsaran Geril's horse rode half a dozen well-fed lamas. They wore orange togas and helmet-shaped hats.

Then came the hearse itself—a low two-wheeled cart drawn by a long-haired Hainak ox. A blue Mongolian cloak, showing the outlines of Tsaran Geril's shrunken form, was spread over the cart. On one side of the cart, at his head, sat old Jeshigema. She sat bent over her dead lord, and every time the springless cart bumped on the uneven ground, she clung to the stiff form and supported its head with the same tender care which she had shown him throughout their life together.

At the tail of the mourning procession rode the little group of old men who were the old caravan leader's kinsmen, the only survivors of a once numerous and proud clan.

When the "casting-out place" was reached the dead man was received by the *haikh-Lama*, who uncovered the naked body. Then all the lamas lifted it from the cart and laid it on the outspread blanket with the head to the northward. Tsaran Geril had grown stiff in a doubled-up position, with his left arm under his head and his right arm in front of his face so that it covered eyes, nose and mouth. This is the coveted "lion's position", which is considered to be a good omen.

Two of the lamas took up a position by the outspread goatskins to intone the five last magic formulas of the *Jyrul*. These are the formulas which dedicate the body to a new life and the released soul to reincarnation in another world. And while this was going on, the snarling of the wild dogs, the shrieks and wing-beats of the birds of prey, mingled with the priests' stream of words and the mourners' cries of grief. The *haikh-Lama* had to hit out on all sides when, to conclude the ceremony, he went to fetch his arrow of death fixed in the earth.

We all hurried off to our nervous horses, and no one looked round as we rode swiftly towards the pass. But long after we had crossed it, the noise from the fighting beasts of prey reached us—a hellish outcry rising from the valley of death, before so silent.

After a stay of a few days in Jeshigema's camp I continued the journey the start of which had been so unexpectedly delayed by my old caravan leader's death. It was a long journey, and several years passed before I was back in the Chahar country.

Of Tsaran Geril's old camping ground only the luxuriant patches of grass remained which showed where he had once had his sheep-folds. I asked in the district what had happened to the inhabitants and heard that they were all dead and " cast out ", and that after the death of the last one the lamas had taken over the whole camp with all its cattle.

Following the impulse of the moment, I tried to get into contact with some of the men of Tsaran Geril's generation, who had travelled, hunted, camped with him ; but I found that they were all dead and their knowledge with them.

All that some few years ago represented the real traditional Mongolia had now disappeared without trace, as much so as the dead themselves. A new generation ruled, a generation which had made no mark so long as the old men still had their place at the camp fires, but which was now active and dominant by virtue of the propaganda injections of the New Time.

Last I rode up to the monastery, and was offered tea in the *haikh-Lama's* cell out of Tsaran Geril's old cup, the cup I had so often seen in the old man's hands when he revealed the secrets of the steppe to me in song or speech—the cup from which on festive occasions he had invited me to drink the crystal-clear kumiss.

The *haikh-Lama* understood what I wished, and Tsaran Geril's cup became mine. When I take up the shallow smoke-blackened birch-wood cup, it is like a good friend's hand-clasp : each of its veins and knots is a golden memory, and the silver-mounted lines and figures recall to me words and thoughts to which it is good to have recourse in evil times.

ROBBER LIFE IN MONGOLIA

ONE of the best known songs in Southern Mongolia is the song about the robber chief Su-mu-ling, the most dreaded and most notorious of all the bandit chiefs who in the years from 1920 to 1935 laid waste and plundered in the South Mongolian frontier regions.

The words of the song tell of one of Su-mu-ling's countless misdeeds in the Chahar country. It happened at a time when the country was in greater distress than it had been for centuries.

The Chinese Republic had lost its control and authority over the possessions lying outside the Great Wall of China which it had inherited in 1912 from the overthrown Manchu dynasty. The inaccessible frontier regions between China and Mongolia had for centuries been the resort of horse-thieves and bandits, but gradually, as these districts slipped outside the reach of the law under the weak regime of the Republic, they became equally a refuge for many of the Chinese evil-doers who had come into collision with the authorities in their own country.

Lawless men settled in the remotest mountain valleys, or along the southern border of Mongolia, where they formed small agricultural colonies. Many married the widows and daughters of poor nomads, as these could support the hard life of the wild better than the Chinese women. It was a rigorous life these men had to live, and in the many years in which the harvest of the lean soil failed they collected in bands and pillaged the richly laden caravans that crossed the frontier mountains on their journeys between China and Central Asia. In certain periods the bands of outlaws became so daring that all communication between China and Mongolia was made impossible.

Imperial Russia exploited the Chinese Republic's powerlessness to its own profit, and in the years between 1912 and 1919 Russian authorities and business houses secured for themselves the whole of the influence in Mongolia which officially was China's due. In the last-named year the Soviet revolution had reached Siberia, and its waves washed in noisily and devastatingly over the once so peaceful steppe country. Bands of Red and White Guards fought out their bitter struggle on the steppes of Mongolia. The mad Baron Ungern hanged those whose opinions differed from his on the curved corners of the temple roofs. Monasteries and camps were plundered of everything transportable; innocent blood flowed in streams; the survivors fled into the isolation of the high mountains, and wolves collected in packs in the footsteps of the ravaging soldiery.

Few of those who went through this hell succeeded in escaping to the coast; but the rumours of the "black years" spread through old channels, and the inhabitants of China again began to speak of their Great Wall as the bulwark of civilization against the foreign barbarians. When the storm had at last passed over the Mongolian steppes, both old Russian and Chinese authorities had been swept away. All the old business houses and trading families had either been extirpated or had fled, and their goods, and all the capital which the country's own wealth represented, had become an object of contention for rival robber bands.

Such were the conditions in Mongolia when in 1923 I approached its frontiers for the first time. The frontier town of Kalgan has neither before nor since contained so many Westerners as in those disturbed days. I myself have never seen anything like the pack of European and American adventurers with whom I then enjoyed entertaining intercourse in the Pioneer tavern at Kalgan. They were a choice collection of sensation- and fortune-hunters, who in a mysterious manner always contrived to make their way to the corners of the world where wild adventures were to be expected. They were a tough lot, those young and cheery desperados, men who would stick at nothing.

They could all scatter easily-won money about them, and they all knew how to enjoy everything that money could buy. But none of them had become degenerate in their sinful indulgence, for for all of them daring adventure was the highest of all pleasures. And now this gang of white men had scented the possibilities of Mongolia and had come to lay hands on all the ownerless riches for which no one dared enter the country. Armed to the teeth, they drove up over the passes and in across the steppes in their modern motor-lorries, to return with rich cargoes of sables, gold and other valuables.

Between their expeditions they poured whisky down their dry throats in the Pioneer tavern at Kalgan, where new stories were continually going the rounds ; and they could tell stories about themselves and their neighbours and anything in the world, however fantastic, without a blush.

There was the American airman who had once been married to a fêted beauty. He was son of one of the leading barristers in New York, and his introduction into this gang of adventurers was due to the world war, his return to find his beauty unfaithful to him, and a last calamitous shot from the revolver he had carried honourably for two years.

There was the deserter from the American marines, who should have gone to school in Texas, but had to make his mark by way of signature. He was burly, red-haired and smiling—with his Irish father's hot blood and his French mother's temperament, which made him invincible in fight. And there were one or two shady characters, like the little French cocaine dealer who lamented the bad times until he came to understand his surroundings and established an agency for whisky.

They had all long ago put themselves outside the pale of civilization ; many of them were wanted by the police of different countries, but I do not think that a single one of these grinning pirates was ever worried by pangs of conscience. They drank and swore, they came and went between the Pioneer tavern at Kalgan and the out-of-the-way corners of the wilderness. They braved all its dangers, snapped up all its chances, and when these had been fully exploited, disappeared to new danger zones—some of them richer, all of them with fresh adventures to relate at fresh bars, and all without having learnt a single one of the many real lessons of the wild.

Only a few of them thought it wisest to make themselves invisible for a time in the wildernesses of Central Asia ; but even there one leaves traces, and in the years that followed I crossed their paths time after time.

The American airman came to have several human lives on his conscience ; and it will be long before the merry Hungarian is forgotten in remote Kansu. On his flight westward he lost both his mount and his baggage, and arrived exhausted and destitute at one of the Christian colonies that in those parts collect around the little Catholic chapels, which are visited only yearly or every other year by the Belgian father in distant Kansu who is their pastor.

The Hungarian appeared in these Old Testament-like surroundings with long hair and a beard, put on a spotless white robe, and narrated to the inhabitants Christian stories and legends which showed that he must have a certain acquaintance with the Bible, besides possessing a considerable knowledge of human nature and a lively imagination. He proclaimed himself to be a direct descendant of Jesus Christ. As such he was received, revered and honoured by the native Christians, and as such he will certainly be remembered for years to come, for all the denials and protests of the Belgian father.

The Chinese robbers in the frontier mountains, who could not flee to new hunting-grounds, were now again the only people who disturbed the peace of the caravan routes.

Europeans had again become a rarity in Kalgan, and the few one met were either missionaries or explorers. The Pioneer tavern was desolate and abandoned, and old Duke Larson's house had now become the starting-place for those who sought the wilderness, for here information about the robbers' movements and disposition was to be had. Here, pretty well every day, the dissolution of old robber bands, and the formation of new ones around new chiefs, was under discussion. Before starting from Kalgan, one made a note of what kind of robbers at the moment dominated the country through which one would travel, for there were many kinds of robbers, and the designations under which they were known were still more numerous.

The cautious Chinese traders, who accepted the robber domination as an unavoidable sovereignty in the frontier mountains, gave the robbers polite names such as " the lords of the roads ", or " the men without a master ", while the nomads called the robber bands which infested the steppe *matsei*, which simply means common horse-thieves. The robbers, to describe themselves, used designations like " the elder brothers ", " the red-beards ", " the red spears " and similar fine-sounding names.

Of all these robbers of more or less Chinese origin the authorities in Kalgan said, as a kind of mitigating circumstance, that " they had left their country for their country's

good ", and they were all more or less tolerated. From time to time, when the bandits became too impudent, as many as could be captured without too much trouble and risk were put to death and their heads nailed to the town wall to reassure the alarmed.

But the men the Chinese feared most of all were the bold warriors who followed leaders like Babodjab, Sain-bayer, Pao Tun-ling, Bejing from Mongoldjin and Li Chouw Hsin. All these leaders, as well as their numerous followers, were

Mongols, and were regarded on the steppe as champions of its freedom. They were welcome guests of honour in all Mongol tents, and they confined their ravages to the Chinese settlers who were ploughing the soil of Mongolia.

From these desperate fighters for freedom we Westerners had nothing to fear, and my friendship with most of them has endured through many years. They were all people whom the Chinese authorities had declared outlaws because they had resisted the occupation of their hereditary grazing-lands by the Chinese. They all fought boldly and bravely in the conviction that fate had marked them out for a violent death.

As the years passed, a new generation of half-breeds became dominant in the Mongolian-Chinese frontier regions. Well-armed deserters from the Chinese army joined up with the worst elements in the frontier mountains, and Su-mu-ling gradually secured for himself the leadership of these bands. It has never been clearly ascertained whether Su-mu-ling was a Chinese or a Mongol, but presumably he, as well as most of his following, belonged to the half-breed class which as a rule inherits the worst characteristics of both sides.

It is known that he grew up in the Chahar country, where as a boy he worked as a shepherd for the stern Lodou chief, and it is declared that Su-mu-ling behaved with so much cruelty in Chahar because, as a boy, he had been badly treated by its chief.

When I came to Mongolia, Su-mu-ling and his savage hordes had for six long years been ravaging the sanctuaries of the country and plundering its camps. He had carried off the country's wealth in cattle and horses, violated its free-born nomad women, mowed down in unequal battle the Mongol warriors disarmed by the authorities at Kalgan; and there were many indications that the Chahar tribe was on the verge of complete ruin.

The song about Su-mu-ling, both words and tune, was composed by the chief's son Banche as he lay dying on the steppe at the foot of the " Blue Mountain ". I have heard the story of the song's origin from the three Mongols who were with Banche at this time—the three who heard him sing:

Brothers, comrades in war, three friends, you must return home quickly,
tell my people what evil has just overtaken me,
and send this greeting to my wife :
If a bird flutters into the abyss, its young still remains ;
My soul will hover cautiously about the tent fire.
Send a greeting to the chief, my brother :
I shall return to earth to see this robber killed,
Su-mu-ling ! my spirit will hover about thee
like a black bird of vengeance.

Banche's three comrades escaped with this last message of his, and they carried the song over the steppes, where it quickly became the most popular and the most often sung of all the beautiful songs in the country. Banche's three comrades gave me the following account of the battle of the Blue Mountain.

The Chahar chief Damarin Surong, in his extremity, had sent a message to the commandant begging for arms to enable the Mongols to defend themselves against Su-mu-ling and his robbers. But the Chinese commandant, who feared armed Mongols much more than Chinese robbers, had only sent them eighteen primitive muzzle-loaders.

Damarin Surong, in his desperate position, had handed over these firearms to eighteen young Mongol volunteers and made Banche, his popular younger brother, leader of the little band of guerillas. This small party of Mongols, on their swift horses, succeeded in carrying out a number of raids on Su-mu-ling's robber band ; but its scanty ammunition supply diminished quickly, and in the battle of the Blue Mountain it came to an end. Only the three who told the story had managed to escape, and the Mongols were again without weapons in face of Su-mu-ling's numerous and well-armed horde.

The battle of the Blue Mountain was only one of Su-mu-ling's many victories in Southern Mongolia, and the death of Banche and his fourteen comrades was apparently an everyday occurrence in this unhappy country, where so many nomads daily fell victims to the robbers.

But the chief's son Banche, who fell in this encounter, and the song he composed in his last hour, will find a place in the history of the Chahar Mongols ; for Banche's heroic death awoke slumbering forces and ideals in the dispirited population, and his song became the steppe's hymn of freedom, which kept the thought of vengeance alive and a real force. It became the song which the Mongolian caravaners were most often heard singing when they dreamed of what lay nearest their hearts, under twinkling stars, to the inspiring accompaniment of the camel bells. Everywhere in the grey felt tents men talked of the battle of the Blue Mountain and recalled to one another the old nomad traditions for which Banche had died a hero's death.

Su-mu-ling and his savage bands continued to dominate Mongolia by violence for many years, but no one who followed the life of the camps could any longer think that the Chahar Mongols were about to collapse. The Chahar people had lost its former privileges and wealth, but among the younger generation there had sprung up a kind of sub-conscious readiness for action, a fount of strength which was derived from the oldest and best traditions of the country.

The Chahar Mongols, who had once had the privilege of belonging to the Manchu emperors' bodyguard, and had been more loyal to the old Peking Government than any of the other tribes of Mongolia, saw at last that no help was to be expected from the Republican Government, which had first disarmed them and later refused them help in their just conflict against lawless oppressors. Year after year the Chahar tribe moved farther north to seek contact with the independent Sunit Mongols. Their daring patrols laid ambushes for the robbers, or they raided Chinese outposts to get themselves arms and ammunition, and the young men collected under the leadership of the old fighters for freedom to prepare themselves for the day of liberation and revenge.

Those who sympathized with the nomads could not fail to note their growing belief in liberation and their will to victory. But all that was noticed in China was that the Chahar Mongols were moving northward, and the robbers' outrages were ignored ; for, after all, it was they who prepared the way for the growing stream of Chinese settlers who year after year ploughed up new areas of the virgin steppe soil, and so enabled the governor at Kalgan to extract more and more in taxation.

Su-mu-ling, in his seemingly victorious advance northward, became increasingly ruthless and arrogant. In 1931 he established himself as commandant in the settlement town of Chapser without anyone disputing the authority he had conferred on himself, and he even came to a kind of agreement with the governor at Kalgan for the sharing of the country's mounting revenue from taxation.

But Su-mu-ling, the great border robber—" the slim beautiful dragon ", he now called himself—did not attain the rich, carefree old age which he anticipated. For in that same year the Japanese occupied Manchuria, and that was the sign for the Mongols to let loose the black bird of vengeance of which Banche had prophesied in his last hour.

Su-mu-ling had to ride out on to desert tracks again, but this time not as a devastating persecuting robber chieftain. With the panic-stricken remnants of his once so savage horde, he fled from his accumulated treasures and sought refuge in the hiding-places of his youth in the frontier mountains. Here in 1935 he met with the death he had so many times deserved.

The effect of Su-mu-ling's death was that the old Chinese robber life came to an end in Inner Mongolia. The old Chahar pastures once more rang with galloping horse-hooves as Sain-bayer, Pao Tun-ling and the other old liberators, with their young nomad warriors, drove the Chinese out of the country, and in 1936 the Great Wall of China again became the frontier between ploughed fields and open steppes.

I have sat by the victorious Sain-bayer's camp fire, and we have listened together to his warriors' mournful songs. That which was most often sung was the song about Su-mu-ling ; for, the old Mongol leader declared, it was the inspiration of the hero Banche in his last hour which gave birth to this fight for freedom which had saved the tribe from ruin.

ON CHRISTIAN SOIL IN A HEATHEN LAND

ON an April day in 1927 my caravan was fighting its way forward against a howling sandstorm. Two of our twenty-four camels had collapsed from exhaustion the day before, and those which remained were so weak that we scarcely dared halt for fear that we should never get them on their legs again.

We had come far into the Durbet chief's barren domains on our way to the Mongolian monastery of Batkhalag, where we had our assembly camp, and from whence the assembled expedition would soon set out on its long journey westward.

Suddenly I caught sight of some outlines which for a moment enticed me away from the big leading camel in whose lee I was struggling along.

Here, a couple of hundred miles or so north of the Blue City, in a desert so barren that it heard nothing but the voices of the caravaners who hastened through it, lay the ruins of a large town, which had certainly been the centre of a rich agricultural population. Outside the ruined town walls there were plain traces of irrigation canals, and everywhere were to be seen millstones, stone mortars and ornamented

ON CHRISTIAN SOIL IN A HEATHEN LAND

blocks of granite, which had once been the foundations of houses.

As I tore myself away to overtake the caravan, which was about to disappear in the sandstorm, I perceived in one of the inside corners of the town wall a number of large blocks of granite, all cut in the form of sarcophagi. On the fronts of these sarcophagus-like blocks of granite crosses were cut, and on their upper sides were spiral-shaped Estrangelo[1] inscriptions which were strange to me.

There was a fascination about the whole of this dead city, and I felt myself rooted to the spot, with a feeling that if I could lift the veil of mystery which centuries had thrown over the place, a great experience would be in store for me.

But as I hurried through the falling darkness after the sound of bells, now growing faint, from my departing caravan, I did not guess that the men who had once worked here, and now slept under the gravestones adorned with crosses, had also listened to the guiding sound of bells, but of quite a different kind.

The expedition continued its long course, and the years that followed brought with them many other experiences and many other tasks; but there were hours too in which I pondered over the mystery of the dead city which I had entered at the beginning of the journey.

While I was exploring in the mountain chains of Tibet and the oases of Turkestan, other white men were finding traces of antiquity in the frontier regions outside the Wall of China. A quantity of bronze signet rings, which were found in the Ordos desert south-west of the Blue City, all bore a cross, and a German scholar discovered north of the Blue City a single sarcophagus-like granite block, ornamented and written on in the same manner as the gravestones which I had seen in my dead city. He established that the inscription was Syrian, and not Mongolian, as I had supposed.

These discoveries helped to localize and confirm a number

[1] An archaic form of the Syriac alphabet.

ON CHRISTIAN SOIL IN A HEATHEN LAND

of statements in the manuscripts of Marco Polo and other mediæval travellers in Asia, and it was thought that the real background had been found for the most mysterious of all the fantastic stories which had reached Europe from unknown Central Asia.

Our European ancestors believed in a powerful Christian ruler, who governed great Christian hordes in distant Tartary. So firm was this belief that the Popes of Rome and the emperors of the Franks sent out men to find this remote Christendom, and the Crusaders never ceased to hope that the Christian ruler would ride out of the eastern darkness to help them in their struggle with the Mohammedan Turks. The mysterious ruler was called Prester John, Presbyter John, or Priest-King John, and the name of his Christian people, it was declared, was the Keraits.

It is hard to say what adequate reasons the European Crusaders had for their confidence in the arrival of help from Central Asia ; but we know that Marco Polo, in his incomparable description of Asia, says that he met a chief who, with a part of his people, belonged to the Nestorian Christian sect and declared himself to be a grandson of Presbyter John. This chief, who called himself King George, met Marco Polo in a village which the latter calls Tenduc ; the situation of this place has long been the subject of discussion, but without result.

The Canadian historian Martin and the Swede Georg Söderbom, who were both members of my last expedition, did a great deal to clear up this question. Their investigations established that the dead city which I had seen in 1927 was only one of several similar cities whose inhabitants had been Nestorian Christians, using the old Syrian script. There is a sister city to the most southerly of these dead Nestorian cities ; it is now inhabited by Chinese and the Mongols of to-day call it Tokhto. It has been supposed that this name is identical with Marco Polo's Tenduc.

But how did it come about that the Keraits, these Central

Asiatic Tartars, became converted to Christianity, observed the ritual of the old Church and worshipped the White Christ at a time when our northern ancestors were still sacrificing to the gods of Valhalla?

Since it has been established that Presbyter John's Christian kingdom belonged to the Nestorian sect and that it used the old Syrian alphabet, it must be presumed that John and his people had been converted by Nestorian priests; for we know that these priests went on long missionary journeys after the sect had been banned first in Asia Minor and after that in Persia.

But how did these Keraits and the Nestorian Christianity in Central Asia disappear so thoroughly that the only traces of them to be found are their long-dead cities and the gravestones which tell of their deaths? It must be presumed either that they were exterminated by the Tumet Mongols, when these poured down from their old grazing lands in Northern Mongolia, or that they were absorbed into this horde and in the course of time abandoned their Christianity under the influence of the Golden Khan's powerful propaganda for Lamaism.

When the great Swedish missionary organizer Fr. Franzon, on one of his journeys, came to the frontier districts outside the Wall of China, he found a savage country whose people were far more closely bound to a kind of idolatry than any other of the many heathen peoples he had met with on his many missionary expeditions. In 1892 Fr. Franzon knelt on the steppe which had once been Priest-King John's Christian dominions, and his prayer that God might help the hard recalcitrant steppe population led to the foundation of two organizations—the Mongolian Mission, a Swedish undertaking, and the Swedish Alliance Mission (Svenska Alliansmissionen).

In the year 1893 the missionary Emanuel Olsen held a baptism at which eighteen heathens were converted to Christianity. Somewhat later Franzon was able to send out forty-five more missionaries to the regions north of the Great Wall, and before the century was out a little mission paper had been started and many Swedish songs had been translated into the language of the natives.

But then came the Boxer rebellion in China, and ten years after the new missionary activity had begun so promisingly, the great majority of the Swedish missionaries and native converts had had to give their lives for their religion. And so it happened that a small party of Swedish missionaries, in flight from the Boxers, was overtaken and martyred at a place where centuries ago the Christian church-bells of the Nestorians must have been heard.

The Swedish martyrs' bones were not laid to rest under stones adorned with crosses ; their naked bodies were cast out to be food for the beasts of prey of the wilderness, and only their heads buried in salt against the day when they could be exchanged for the silver which the old Empress Dowager of China had promised for every long-nosed head of a foreign devil.

But no silver was ever paid for this crime. After the Empress Dowager had fled before the foreign troops who came to avenge the Boxers' misdeeds, the murderers of the Swedish missionaries took fright, and before the expedition which had been sent to ascertain the missionaries' fate reached the scene of the crime, the criminals had endeavoured to destroy all traces of it. An old shepherd, however, pointed out the way, and in the ashes of a great fire were found a child's shoe and a long fair plait of hair. The ashes were collected and placed in as many chests as there were murdered missionaries, and all these were buried west of the Blue City.

But the preaching of the Christian religion in the frontier regions north of the Wall of China did not come to an end with the deaths of these martyrs, for new missionaries were soon called to the same field, and new chapels were erected on the burned-down ruins. Their little tinkling bells call unwearyingly to those who bow before splendid images of

Buddha, turn towards Mohammed's Holy City or listen to the dull beat of the Shaman drums.

Now and then it happens that some of the many who have not obtained from the local gods help in their need or consolation in their sorrow listen to the sharp tinkle of the foreigners little bell and join the community which worships the foreigners' God. And if one follows one of these parties of converts, one comes to the Swedish Alliance Mission's station on the edge of the Blue City. The station lies only a few stone's-throws from the house where Tzu Hsi, so renowned for her virtues and vices, spent her childhood—she who as Empress Dowager inspired the Boxer rebellion and caused the deaths of so many Christians.

The little bell which clangs unweariyingly from its narrow chamber is of Swedish origin ; one of the first missionaries brought it with him from his home in Skaane.

The chapel is an oblong building whose whitewashed walls shine out among the grey clay houses of the surrounding quarter. A slender cross gleams from its high roof, as if to support the summons of the bell. Round the chapel are grouped all the small buildings which contain the school, hospital and workshops, where on the six working days of the week there is great activity. Behind is the little dwelling-house which is the home of the missionary Wiberg and his wife out here in the field of work to which they felt themselves called. With its flat roof and yellowish-grey clay walls, it is like many other Chinese houses, but its bright windows diffuse an atmosphere of homely comfort and cheerful happiness which distinguishes it from all the others.

The house is surrounded by a garden ; this now lies in its sound winter sleep, but from the well-kept neatness one can guess how pretty it is in summer. In one corner stands a tall stone with long inscriptions in Chinese, a stately memorial to Colonel Chao, who was sent by the Peking Government in 1914 to combat the many bandits of the district. Chao carried out his task so well that the Government made him

ON CHRISTIAN SOIL IN A HEATHEN LAND

a general, and the inscription on the stone is his own testimony that the cause of his success was his having been baptized on that spot.

The little bell goes on calling, and the community streams in through the wide open doors of the chapel. The congregation distributes itself over the narrow benches on each side of the central aisle. They are all clean and smartly dressed, and all regard me with a stereotyped but certainly well-intended grin.

At the end of the central aisle stands a tall wooden lectern draped with red silk, and with signs representing Biblical words in Chinese sewn onto it.

The congregation consists of about sixty Chinese. Men and women sit separately, each sex on one side of the central aisle. The women are in a majority, and the congregation consists mainly of elderly people. Some of them are old enough to have been through the terrifying days of the Boxer rebellion as Christians. And there are many Chinese babies dressed in red, sitting safely on their mothers' knees. They are the mission's hope for the future.

Fru Wiberg takes her place at the little Swedish organ, and the whole congregation joins in a hymn.

A tall thin Chinese goes up into the pulpit ; his eyes suggest that he has wonderful experiences to relate. This is Pastor Wang, the most learned and respected member of the Christian community. He seeks and holds the eyes of all the congregation, and then explains the text of the Bible in the language he would use, and the manner he would assume, if he were telling them about something he himself had seen the day before in the nearest town. His words are so fascinating, the play of his features so eloquent, the people he describes so home-like, and their experiences so marvellous, that even the children can follow him, and everyone forgets that he is speaking of the foreigners' God.

Pastor Wang's father was one of the mission's first Christians and one of the few who survived the Boxer persecution. He, like others, was knocked about till he was thought to be dead, after which his unconscious body was thrown into the river to float downstream. But the cold water revived him, and he succeeded in swimming ashore under cover of darkness and escaping to a place of safety.

Pastor Wang has finished his sermon, and the faces of the congregation show that they have been convinced of the truth of his words. All bow their heads in deep reverence when it is time to pray, and no one gives a thought to the fact that the Swedish missionary Wiberg has replaced their own Pastor Wang at the altar, for they are all Christians, and they all believe in one common God.

The chapel has emptied, the bell is silent, and the little band of Christians scatters among the multitude who worship the old gods of the place. Will they return in ever greater numbers, or will they be swallowed up and disappear, like the Nestorians before them?

I believe in the power of the little Skaane bell out in the remote wild, and I hope for the fulfilment of the missionary's prayer for his country and people.

THE OASIS BEYOND THE DESERT

THE strange names of distant regions often come into my head in these days when I sit at home. And most of all at this time, when all Nature is full of scent and radiance, and the summer girls combine daring colours in their fluttering dresses.

Thoughts cannot be confined, and mine to-day are dancing out through the wide-open veranda door to frolic among lilacs, laburnums and chestnuts; they listen awhile to the cool gush of the garden hose—and then they creep in among the silky white buds of a proud magnolia, which gleams in the sunshine like the candelabra on a communion table. Thoughts love to dance hand in hand with beautiful memories, and the exotic splendour of a magnolia in flower always recalls to me the same unforgettable scene.

It is just sixteen years since I sat at the foot of the magnolia which stands like a proud minaret in Kurban Beg's Mohammedan pleasure garden. I sat cross-legged on a Khotan carpet as soft as moss and inhaled the gentle aroma from a hookah ornamented with coral and turquoises. The worthy owner of the garden, who was also sheik of the whole oasis, sat at my side to see that I had what I needed, and every wish I expressed was followed by an order to the servants who stood round. The sheik's orchestra sat twelve yards away, producing seductive sleepy notes in perfect harmony with the burning siesta hour. The white-clad slaves offered me in turn golden grapes, roasted nuts, downy peaches, ice-cold yogurt[1] and much else in which the oasis abounded. All the cheerful sounds of life from the bazaars on the other side of the high garden walls had ceased, and gradually the music too died away. For a time I heard only the monotonous clucking and purling from the garden's many watering apparatus . . . I noticed how the gently moving servants kept away the insects with long noiseless strokes of their fans . . . I stretched myself out and plunged all ten fingers into dewy luxuriant grass. . . . It was a delicious siesta with wonderful dreams—that first sleep of mine in the "oasis beyond the desert".

I had come to the "oasis beyond the desert" that very morning after a journey of more than three months through the notorious Taklamakan. It is affirmed that all other deserts are tame in comparison with Taklamakan; but the mighty powers of the desert had only revealed themselves to me—they had never been able to cast me down. We had often to cling to the tent-posts while the *kara buran*, the "black storm", ploughed through the sea of sand; we had seen the young camels sink down exhausted only a few miles from the water-hole that meant salvation. And I had heard the caravan men grumbling ceaselessly about our certainly having lost our way and this marvellous oasis being one of the creatures of my imagination.

But I knew that the oasis existed, because four Europeans

[1] Sour milk.

THE OASIS BEYOND THE DESERT

in all had visited it before me and lived to tell the tale. The first of these was the Venetian Marco Polo, who passed through the oasis on his famous journey to Kanbalu more than six centuries ago. Much later the Russian Przhevalski came to it, and finally, at the end of the last and the beginning of this century, Sven Hedin and Sir Aurel Stein. And all four told the same story of the remote oasis, its isolated inhabitants and the vast, formidable country that surrounded it. But their accounts—which agreed with one another—at the same time contained much which gave an attractive picture of a harmonious little community which, owing to its almost total isolation from the changing world outside, had continued to live the life of an age long past in Old Testament-like peace and happiness.

Three months in a barren desert, empty of life; always the same breathless silence, broken only by the sudden furious onslaughts of the " black storms " ; by night the stars and mysterious noises ; and always the same feverish striving to reach the next watering-place.

How explain the fact that he who has had the desert for his pillow longs and longs to get back to it ? Is it the everlasting struggle with the unforeseen which attracts him? Is it the playing with dangers, or the unforgettable hours in which one feels oneself an inseparable part of almighty Nature, the seconds in which one is allowed one sudden swift glimpse of truths till then unsuspected, uncomprehended ? I do not know—yet ; I only know that one cannot help longing and longing to get back. But we do all know that one needs to have been really hungry and thirsty to enjoy a well-loaded table to the full.

Hunger and thirst were done with for this time ; we had really reached the land of plenty. Already, when two days' marches from the oasis, we had been received by a welcome committee consisting of six of the " whitebeards " of the oasis, who bowed to the sand and called me Excellency, begging me to partake of the refreshments they had brought with them.

These consisted of everything which of late had ceaselessly haunted my thoughts and dreams ; and they were offered in such abundance that they almost hid the pattern of the large embroidered carpet that lay spread out on the sand.

And while the six " whitebeards " treated me with all the ceremonious politeness of the East, which to these " worthies " represented the warmest cordiality, their servants looked after me and my caravan men and watered my camels.

When at last we started, the people from the oasis accompanied us as guides, and when at sunset we sighted the green trees and white minarets of the oasis we were met by a new deputation, which received us with tents ready pitched, food and refreshments. Next morning they mounted me on a fresh desert horse, and we covered the last short lap to the " oasis beyond the desert " at a cheerful gallop. In the cool belt of shade which the outermost trees cast upon the yellow desert sand, Kurban Beg stood amid a group of other white-bearded, turbaned men to welcome the desert traveller to their oasis. In elegant phrases and charming language they said everything a mother, sweetheart or sister could say at her dear one's homecoming from a long and difficult journey. They even said that the whole oasis and all it contained was mine for as long as I wished to honour it with my presence.

Then I was conducted to the sheik's pleasure garden, where I was again entertained in princely fashion. I had for the first time fully experienced the joy it is for the traveller in the desert to arrive at an oasis. Who else but a desert people could, in so limited a space, have thought out and conjured up such an abundance of ingenious arrangements, which so completely distracted one's thoughts from the sea of sand that surrounded them ? Everywhere in the sheik's garden there were shady places commanding beautiful luxuriant views ; broad-leaved trees gave protection against the burning sun and the hot desert wind ; wherever I sat or stood, I could hear the bubbling water in the fountains and irrigation canals ; the greenness of the vegetation and the gay colours of the flowers shone out brightly in the softened light of the garden.

When I awoke from my pleasant doze, the hour of the siesta was over, and the cheerful noises which reached me from the bazaars on the other side of the high garden walls told me that the oasis was coming to life again. I lay for a while and absorbed the wonderful spirit of the place.

The garden began to be full of life and activity. The sheik approached, heading a slow procession of servants and slaves, who immediately set to work on the innumerable preparations which herald an Asiatic feast. A low red-lacquered table was placed upon the carpet within my reach. A party of men arrived dragging a couple of bleating fat-tailed sheep; the sheik felt the animals and found them young and fat, whereupon they were slaughtered and placed upon spits over a newly-kindled fire. Musicians with queer stringed instruments and tambourines again took their places under the scented mulberry trees, and immediately began tuning the strings and warming the tight-stretched skin of the tambourines.

The red-lacquered table began to groan under copper dishes of fruit and sweetmeats, and on the other side of it a large embroidered carpet was spread. The participators in the feast began to arrive; they bowed and stroked their long beards as a mark of respect to the sheik and his white guest, and then sat down in a large circle round the outspread carpet. The whitebeards sat nearest the table, the blackbeards farther off, according to age and rank, and the downy-chinned youths sat at the opposite end of the circle. All wore large, freshly ironed muslin turbans, long white coats with many folds, and soft embroidered riding-boots. The servants brought hookahs and placed them before their masters; a light veil of smoke soon hung over the scene of the feast, and the delicate aroma of tobacco mingled with the strong smell of roasting meat from the sheep over the fire.

The servants began to hand round to the guests Chinese

cups of steaming tea, and the hookahs were put aside to cool. Some of the youngest and least dignified began to cast glances at the fire, where two half-naked perspiring men stood turning the spits on which the sheep were being roasted whole. These were now done brown and dripped blood and fat which made the fire spurt and crackle. The smell of roasting meat was so strong that the guests could not help licking their lips and wiping the saliva from their chins. They began to turn up the sleeves of their long coats and play with their long knives. And at last feeding time came. At a sign from the sheik the first sheep was carried along and flung into a large wooden trough in the midst of the circle of hungry men. Then the sheik clapped his hands, and all rose to call down Allah's blessing on the meal which was to be eaten.

Then the sheik approached the sheep and with practised hand divided it into large lumps, which were carried round to the guests. The guest of honour was served first and got the best bits; I was also served first with white wine from home-grown grapes out of great ice-cold clay bottles.

The Koran forbids a believer to indulge in any form of alcohol, but I soon found that the form of Mohammed's religion which this isolated community observed was much more tolerant and pleasant than that of the other followers of the Prophet. The freshly roasted mutton was underdone and juicy, the wine was sweet and cold as ice, and the delicious fruits which were eaten between the courses stimulated the appetite. The music struck up, a singer stepped forward, and the guests began to belch from sheer well-being and civility. The embroidered carpet was cleared of bones and fragments of food, the music changed over to a steadier measure, and the sheik clapped his hands again.

Seven veiled forms glided in as noiselessly as moonbeams. The sheik with a motion of his hand ordered them to sit down on the embroidered Khotan carpet which marked my place of honour. They were tall and slim, and wore long silk embroidered flame-coloured robes. They had on their heads little velvet caps trimmed with gold and silver ; these kept in place long muslin veils which hid their faces. They spread around them an atmosphere of purity and exotic perfume, and for the first time in many years I had an instinctive feeling that I had fascinating young women about me.

The music continued to play vague wandering tunes, of which the tambourines did their level best to mark the rhythm. The hookahs had been set to work again, and the light puffs of smoke from them combined to weave a fairy veil which hovered to and fro over the wide embroidered carpet.

The last lingering daylight had given way to the flickering gleam of the fire ; a light evening breeze from the desert blended all the strong scents of the garden into one strange aroma, which made one feel that one was on the threshold of a delightful adventure. I glanced at the veiled forms which surrounded me. They sat quite motionless except that their little crimson velvet slippers had begun to move in time with the jingling of the tambourines. They were tiny little gold-trimmed slippers with pointed turned-up toes on which were big yellow velvet pompoms. These must be women !

The flickering fire light began to play upon the flame-coloured silk robes, and I discovered that the wearers had noticed my interest. In their muslin veils were small oblong openings through which their eyes looked, and their eyes were black and sparkling and fixed on me. The sheik moved over to my side, and after caressing his long white beard for a time, he began to whisper in my ear :

" These girls are from Nija ; one of them is so clean and pure that her slender neck becomes purple when she drinks the red Turfan wine. If you choose her, you will stay with us for a long time."

I knew this Sartish phraseology and what it signified. I wondered which of the seven girls it was who was " as beautiful as a goddess ". Except for their little caps, which were of different coloured velvet, they were all dressed exactly alike ;

they had the same tall slim figures, the same grace and the same sparkling eyes. But all seven of them were from Nija, and the girls from Nija have long been considered the most delicious of all the pretty girls in Turkestan. It was maidens from Nija who in the old days were sent as tribute to the Emperor in distant Peking. Now there was no longer any Emperor to whom costly gifts could be sent ; now Turkestan's treasures remained in Turkestan, in whose markets one could pick up three Nija beauties for one moderately good donkey—and so seven of them had been brought to the " oasis beyond the desert ".

After long observation and consideration I came to the conclusion that the girl in the blue cap must be she whom the sheik had praised.

The orchestra's stringed instruments fell into harmony with the tambourines, and the circle of men accompanied the tune with hand-clapping to mark the rhythm. The sheik gave a cry ; a singer advanced into the middle of the circle, and the girls from Nija sprang up to form a circle round him. And now the feast in Kurban Beg's pleasure garden in the cool of the night woke to hot life. For a while the girls stood and took little steps in time with the melody ; their slim hands moved in the air and finally were clasped behind their necks ; and then they flung themselves into the dance.

They were not paid dancing girls. The dancing of the girls from Nija was the physical expression of joy of youth and grace and delight in rhythm : themselves carried away by the music, they carried away the circle of men, whose warm admiration stimulated them to ever higher achievements.

After each dance the singer went round among the guests of honour to distribute long silk ribbons of the same colour as the girls' caps, and as I had first pick every time, I could always get the colours of the girl of my choice. My chosen Nija girl was delicious, much more supple and graceful than the red and the yellow, or any of the other dancers ; and as after a dance each girl had to sit beside the man who had chosen the ribbon of her colour, she became my regular partner between the dances.

And while she cleaned and lighted my hookah, poured wine into my cup, stuffed grapes and almonds into my mouth and cared for my well-being in a variety of other ways, I had an opportunity of studying her more closely. At first she coloured bashfully when I raised her muslin veil, but then a smile lit up her face, and I saw that her eyes could grow warm and velvety, and that her slim fingers were made for caresses.

All night my blue Nija girl danced for me, and between the dances she listened bright-eyed to my vinous chatter. When the last dance was over, and the tambourines and stringed instruments were silent, she remained at my side until the new day lit up Kurban Beg's garden with the soft hues of the dawn. In silence we saw the growing radiance of the rising sun clothe the blossoms of the fruit trees in warm colours. Tens of thousands of dewdrops made peaches, apricots and grapes sparkle like jewels in a scene from fairyland. And while the herons rose from their colony in the oasis and sailed off with noiseless wing-beats to one of the reed-bordered salt lakes of the desert, she related to me the many events of her young life. She told of her long journey from Nija to the " oasis beyond the desert ", of sand-drifts and " black storms ", of the wild beasts of the mountains and the wild camels of the desert. And she told of all the evil spirits of the desert, whose presence I had vaguely felt, but of which she had actual experience—of ghostly caravans which passed the camps at night, and voices by day which tried to entice the traveller away from his course. She had often heard the voices of her dear ones calling to her from the desert, and several times singing and beautiful dance music had tried to lead her away into the sea of sand. And last she told of her arrival at the " oasis beyond the desert ", which had been only four days before my own. The " oasis beyond the desert ", where she felt just as strange, but just as welcome and happy as I myself.

A week later I was sitting on the verge of the desert watching an unforgettable sunset. My camels were wandering among the tamarisks on the edge of the oasis and gorging on the cactus-like grass which is their favourite food. They had already recovered considerably, and lifted their long necks to gaze out into the desert with unfathomable eyes.

I often let my eyes wander southward, up to the snow-powdered slopes and ice-clad peaks of the Tibetan frontier mountains.

As I sat there, wondering what lay hidden on the other side of the high passes in the " land of snow ", one of my servants came bringing me a present. I had become quite accustomed to receive presents in this idyllic oasis, but the little bag's contents were most peculiar. It contained a small piece of charcoal, a withered flower, a hawk's feather and a walnut. I turned to the messenger in astonishment to ask him whence this curious present came, and he replied with a broad grin that the letter to the Sahib was from the girl from Nija. " Letter ? " I asked in bewilderment, for there was really no letter, but the servant continued to smile as he pointed to the bag's contents.

I put the little piece of charcoal, the withered flower, the hawk's feather and the walnut back into the bag and went to the sheik for an explanation. When the worthy man saw the contents of the bag, he laughed so much that his long white beard shook, and when at last he was able to speak, it was only to say that I should live a very long time in the " oasis beyond the desert ".

When at last he realized that I understood nothing, he laid his arm about my shoulder and said, pointing at the four objects one by one :

" The message to you from the Nija girl is this : The flames of love consume me . . . if I had wings I would fly to thee . . . I give myself to thee."

That evening I ordered a start to be made next morning, and as we set our course at dawn for Wild Goat Pass, which gives entrance to the high snows of Tibet, I looked back for the last time. I saw a magnolia towering like a proud minaret above mulberry trees in flower ; its silky white buds shone in the sunshine like candelabras on the altar of love—a tempting exotic altar, but beyond my reach.

IN THE LAND OF SNOW

IN two of the four seasons of the year the water-laden monsoon winds sweep over burning, sweating India—and nature is transformed as by the stroke of an enchanter's wand. The whole tropical plant world takes a bound forward and grows up in miraculous fashion, and the elephants' delighted trumpeting and the monkeys' cheerful chatter rise from the moist virgin forests and jungles.

The luxuriance which the monsoon brings to the people of India is full of fever, and every year hundreds of thousands are killed by the plague and other epidemics which the sea winds bring in their train.

But as the monsoon winds sweep arrogantly northward they suddenly run their heads into a stone barrier which forces them upward higher and higher, and presses and squeezes them till all the moisture they have brought with them is turned into ice and snow, and this falls to the earth again.

IN THE LAND OF SNOW

The country over which these masses of snow fall has been given the name Himalaya, the land of snow. Himalaya has further been called the roof of the world, since it is a part of the highest mountain system in the world, and its dominating peaks rise into the sky twice as high as the highest mountain in Europe. Mount Everest, Gauri Sankar and Nanga Tarbat are names given by men to some of these giants of nature, so immensely high that in favourable weather they can be sighted by the perspiring human multitudes right down in the pestilential swamps of Hindustan. Their snow-white purity and imposing majesty are full of charm and fascination, and when the peaks, bright with glaciers, are turned to gold by the sun, the natives throw themselves on the ground in spontaneous reverence.

But the sun does not shine every day in the Himalayas; the land of snow is also the home of storms. When the god of the winds loosens the mouth of his sack, all the freezing winds of the north rush down over Central Asia, until they too run their heads into the Himalayas' compact mountain masses. Howling and whining they press through the narrow passes, tear and shake the snow on the mountain ridges, flinging avalanches of ice and snow down into the valleys, and assault the snow-covered peaks, till nothing is seen but an opaque inferno of drifting white masses of snow. It is these snow-storms, exterminating all life, and the immense height of the country, which make the flora and fauna of the snow regions so scanty; and these also supply the reason why the central parts of the Himalayas are almost uninhabited.

The Himalayas are a huge, almost insurmountable barrier between the old culture States of India and all the rest of European Asia. In the midst of the snows the frontiers of three world Powers meet—those of Russia, Great Britain and China—but this frontier region is so savage and inimical to life that it is both impossible and superfluous to guard it.

None the less there are a number of tracks which connect the countries to north and south, for there are and always have been people with an uncontrollable desire to see the unknown on the other side of the mountain passes. Centuries before our era began, these tracks were trodden by Alexander the Great and his Macedonians with their silver shields; and both Jenghiz Khan's Mongolian bowmen and Tamerlane's Tartar horsemen followed them at intervals of centuries to gaze upon the splendours of India. The Hellenistic form of art came to India with the Macedonians and there gave birth to the Gandara style, while, on the contrary, Buddhism, in our day the most widespread of all religions, reached Central Asia and China over the difficult tracks of the snow lands.

These tracks, over which such important cultural messages were spread, and along which some of the world's greatest statesmen and conquerors have hastened to the assault, are to-day just as difficult and primitive as when they were trampled up by Alexander's Macedonians thousands of years ago.

But there is a kind of man different from those who storm barriers to loot the wealth which is hidden on the other side; and it is in such men's company that I myself have travelled in the land of snow.

My journey began thus. In the spring of 1930 I left Tientsin on board an American tourist steamer bound for Vancouver. I came straight from a long caravan journey through the plateau of Asia and had let myself be persuaded to make a trip to America to enjoy that continent's civilization. The steamer was luxuriously equipped throughout and full of Americans who thoroughly understood how to enjoy luxury. Before the ship set her course eastward to cross the great Pacific Ocean, we called at the greatest of all Eastern Asiatic ports and there collected new crowds of tourists, who herded together at the bar to try out all the thrilling stories soon to be retailed to friends and acquaintances in the " old country ".

Calcutta was the last Asiatic port on the trip, and we were

to lie there three days to take on board water, fuel and provisions. It was in the middle of the monsoon period, and at midday I fled from the blazing hot, noisy, bazaar streets into the massive stone building of the Calcutta Museum to find shade and quiet. I was wandering slowly through rooms in which the objects exhibited carried messages from all the remarkable countries of the world, when I suddenly stopped dead at the sound of a soft humming which reminded me of a tune I had often heard in quite different surroundings—and long ago.

I had to stand still for a moment to make sure I really heard it; then I followed the sound—in through the door to the right—and all of a sudden I was back in Mongolia. In one corner of a large room, whose walls were hung with Central Asiatic draperies, stood a Mongolian tent, and it was from this that the Mongolian sounds emanated. It was the song about homesickness that is so often sung by the hunters and shepherds of Mongolia—perhaps because their lives so frequently take them far from home.

When I bent down cautiously towards the opening of the tent, I saw through its embroidered frame something which made me forget India's moist heat, the hectic noise from the bazaar streets outside, and the artificial environment of the museum. Bent over a low table sat my old Mongol friend Biliktai, in whose Spartan monk's cell I had so often sought a night's lodging. He had exchanged his orange lama's cloak for the white toga-like coat which the Indian Buddhists wear, but he had the same lined face and eyes tired with much reading as when I visited him in the remote Urga monastery. As then, the butter lamp burned on the altar table at his side; as then, he was busily engaged in writing graceful Mongolian characters on large sheets of rice paper; and as then, he was humming one of the melancholy steppe songs as he worked.

When I crossed the low threshold of the tent I felt that I was walking straight into Mongolia. Our pleasure at meeting again was great and genuine. Questions and answers followed, and these joined up and expanded into stories; and when the museum clock recalled us to realities, we knew all about each other's doings since the day when we had last seen one another more than six years before.

In 1924 Biliktai had been at Urga studying the mystical doctrine of the Tantra religion, and he had had to flee from Northern Mongolia when it was occupied by the Soviet in 1925. He had covered the 750 miles to Kalgan on his riding camel, and had gone on with a Turkmen caravan to Yarkand in distant Kashgaria. He had later joined a party of Torgut pilgrims bound for holy Lhasa, and had continued his pilgrimage alone to Budh Gaya in India to see the place where Gotama Buddha had received " enlightenment ".

The last part of the long journey had exhausted Biliktai both bodily and financially, and he had ended up as a wreck, shivering with fever, in the Calcutta mission hospital. No one understood his language in this foreign place, and he himself did not understand a word of the dialects he heard around him.

But one day a white man came to see him who understood, and could make himself understood in, Tibetan, of which language Biliktai, as an erudite lama, also had a fair knowledge. And when his illness had run its course, his new friend found work for him on the arrangement of the Mongolian collections in the museum.

It was more than a year since he had conversed with anyone in his native language, and still longer since he had heard any news from the cool steppes of his homeland. In the days that followed we talked much of the life of the steppes and the atmosphere of the wild, and on the third day we began to ask one another about our plans for the future. I told Biliktai about the imposing steamer in which I was to go out on to the high seas next day, of the symbolic meaning of the Statue of Liberty, of the skyscrapers and everything else there was to see in the land of freedom, but my enthusiasm paled quickly in face of the lack of interest which, despite all my efforts, he plainly showed.

We both sat in silence for a long time, till suddenly he asked me : " Why are you really going to the ' land of freedom ' ? " And he began to tell me about his own plans, while I pondered over my answer ; but I soon gave up pondering to listen to his words.

He spoke of the road northward that rises from the tropical forest regions, winds among tree-like ferns, creeps under shady acacias and ascends through woods of pine, oak and cedar. White glacier water roars down the valleys ; sissus, rhododendron and wild roses make the valley slopes splendid with their abundance of scent and colour. We have left tigers and wild elephants behind and are in the realm of mouflon, ibex and wild yak. And now we say farewell to the last primula, which holds its head up bravely on the edge of the eternal snows.

We have risen above all the domains which are inhabited by fighting beasts and men ; we have come into the great silence of the snows, and ahead of us a lonely track leads to the white-powdered peak of Gauri Sankar.

When the American tourist steamer reached Vancouver, Biliktai and I were on the way to Kashmir, and as at the beginning of June the passes had shaken off the worst of the snow, we climbed over the Zooji-la and entered Ladakh. We spent the rest of the summer in the Dongche monastery, situated near the caravan route which leads from Yarkand in Turkestan to Delhi in India. The Dongche monastery can be seen at a great distance, for it was built many centuries ago and—how one cannot understand—round the very peak of a high rock shaped like a pyramid. All the water and provisions needed by the two hundred monks of the monastery have to be dragged up thousands of steps cut in the steep sides of the rock. This laborious task, and all lay duties within the area of the monastery itself, are carried out by young monks and novices in the hours in which they are not occupied with religious studies.

The monastery, the position and appearance of which recall an old robber castle, is famous for its able magicians and healers, who draw to the place pilgrims from the whole Lamaist world. The ever-burning butter lamps in the halls of the temples, the sacrifices and the daily worship are the care of the oldest monks, while the religious needs of the scanty population in the monastery's vast upland area are looked after by elderly but still vigorous monks.

A large number of the monks in the monastery are so old that they will never again set foot on the path which connects them with the outer world; and many are so aged and physically feeble that they cannot leave the cells which in the prime of their youth they took over from old men whose lives were finished. They sit like old eagles huddled up on their hard wooden beds and peer out through the square loop-holes in the strong cell walls. A ceaseless stream of prayers and incantations flows from their toothless gums, while their eyes wander over snow-clad mountain ridges and ice-covered peaks to the highest horizons in the world. It is as though all their thoughts and the whole of their worldly personalities had long cast off the fetters that bind a man to earth.

The road past the monastery, on which no human life had appeared since November in the previous year, came into use again in July. Parties of Mohammedan Turkmenians and Kansu people came along it; since the Soviet had shut its frontiers against all believers, they had to take this dangerous detour to reach their holy Mecca. Buddhist pilgrims too drifted by, on their long journey down to Budh Gaya, where Sukya Muni Buddha received " enlightenment ". By far the greater part of these were old people, and many of them were women, but they marched cheerfully and confidently towards the distant goal which many of them would never reach.

When a snowstorm had raged over the passes to the north, the young monks of the monastery held themselves ready at the foot of the sacred rock to assist the bands of sufferers who would seek refuge there. When these pilgrims had recovered somewhat and received food and medical care, their leader always held a roll-call to ascertain how many had fallen victims to the storm. Dozens often went under in one single snowstorm, and as I rode back along the pilgrims' weary way, I read resigned contentment and transfigured happiness in the stiffened faces.

In August I had one of the greatest surprises of my life. I had been sitting in a reverie oblivious of everything, watching the sun as it fell slowly towards the purple landscape ; I had seen the dark hues of night rise from the depths around me and slowly gather round the highest peaks, till these too were wrapt in darkness.

Suddenly I was aroused from my dreams by Biliktai's hoarse voice. It was clear that his message was of importance, but he had to repeat it several times before I grasped the meaning of his words. A countryman of mine, a *Danmarki hung*, had arrived at the Dongche monastery to see me. Full of doubt and curiosity, I accompanied Biliktai to the guest-house of the monastery to inspect the new arrival. I thought he might be a Russian refugee from Turkestan or a daring English hunter from India.

But Biliktai was right. The young man who hurried forward to meet me was as bronzed as an Indian and as dirty as a Tibetan, but his cheerful greeting was as Danish as could be, and round his waist he wore a broad sash whose red and white colours formed a Dannebrog flag.

This was the first time in his life that Biliktai had heard me talk my own language, and all that night and the days that followed he did not hear me say much that was not in Danish. The new arrival at the Dongche monastery in the far Himalayas was Polycarpus Lindquist, son of a Swedish bootmaker who had settled in Copenhagen. Having come through his school-leaving examination in fine style, he had decided to bicycle round the world and succeeded in getting his enterprise financed by a Copenhagen daily paper, to which he was to send travel articles. He had bicycled from the Raadhusplads through the countries of Europe and Asia to India, where, in Calcutta, he found out that I had been there some months earlier.

Polycarpus's route was to have been from Calcutta through Burma and Siam to China and Japan, but now he bicycled back to Delhi and continued along the old military road northward to Rawalpindi and Srinagar. At Srinagar he heard that I had disappeared into the land of snow, and as his bicycle could be of no use to him there, he exchanged it for mountaineering equipment. So up he came into the mountains, and without an idea of the dangers he was incurring, and without understanding more than a few words, learnt by heart, of the language of the country, he had found me in one of the most remote and inaccessible monasteries in the world.

Polycarpus was one of the most cheerful and pleasant fellows I have ever met; he could shout with joy at the prospect of an adventure, and he could sit silent, plunged in deep and fervent thankfulness for all the beauties of nature which Providence was allowing him to see.

One day, when Polycarpus and I were walking northward along the road to visit a pilgrims' camp which had been overwhelmed by a snowstorm, we met a caravan which had forestalled us. As we were accompanying the caravan and the survivors from the camp back to the monastery, I noticed that some of the pilgrims were of a quite different type from the people one usually met in those parts, and that the language they used when they spoke to one another contained words which reminded me of Mongolian. We succeeded in getting the people to rest at the monastery for a few days, and when these had elapsed, and the caravan had continued its journey southward, I had found out through the circumspect Biliktai that they called themselves Mongols, and where their homeland lay. There was good ground for believing that they were descendants of the Mongol Empress Nukodar's army, whose disappearance more than five hundred years ago, and its subsequent fate, even the Mongols themselves cannot explain.

That evening Polycarpus, Biliktai and I lay on our stomachs in our cell studying a map of the Himalayas, Afghanistan and Turkestan, and in the days that followed we made great plans. It was late in the summer, but if the weather was normal, we had still a couple of months before the passes into the land of snow became impracticable.

A few days later Polycarpus and Biliktai started northward, taking with them all the equipment we had, while I hurried back to Srinagar to get supplies and equipment for a two years' expedition. We counted on meeting at Yarkand before Christmas, and thence we could continue the journey to our destination at our leisure.

A fortnight later a runner brought me a short letter from Polycarpus, and on the following night came a fall of snow which blocked the Zooji-la pass—several weeks earlier than usual—and therewith my way to the camp where Polycarpus lay sick. His letter informed me in brief phrases that he was down with dysentery and needed help.

There was still one possibility of reaching Polycarpus—by making a detour round the Zooji-la pass to westward, over the Burzil and Tragbal passes, which were still open, and then make our way eastward through one of the cross valleys. We got over the Tragbal pass successfully, but the night before we were to ascend Burzil the first snowfall of the winter in that district came. The snow went on falling for three days, and when we continued the ascent on the fourth day it lay piled up many feet high and hung over our heads almost at the angle at which it begins to move and plunges down in avalanches.

We started while the stars were still out, for we wanted to get as high as possible before the sun set the masses of snow moving. Fortunately it was perfectly still, and we picked our way forward in absolute silence, so as not to cause one of those little movements of air which can have such catastrophic results. We climbed higher and higher, and could see that we were already on the saddleback of the pass. We came nearer and nearer to the top of the mountain wall that was on our left, and on our right we had a sheer drop of about 180 feet.

I felt in my left breast pocket for a bit of cheese and looked forward to the cigarette I should enjoy when we reached the top.

But we never reached the top.

A tremendous roar, followed by a cannonade of echoes which rattled among the precipices, announced that an avalanche had fallen in one of the valleys near by, and then all the masses of snow and ice that were piled up round us began to move and roll. Faster and faster they rolled, till they grew into gigantic balls sweeping trees and stones with them into the depths. It was like being in a defenceless small boat right in the line of fire between two mighty fleets.

It may have been hours, perhaps only seconds, before I saw something vast and white rushing towards me, and when at last I was dug out by the survivors, I lay down at the bottom of the valley, and a quantity of broken bones prevented me from moving a single limb. I lay for seventy-two days at the foot of the Burzil pass, deep in the heart of the snow country, before the relief expedition reached me, but then poor Polycarpus had been dead for more than three months, and Biliktai had disappeared without leaving a trace.

But five years later, when I was again on my way to the plateau of Asia, I found Biliktai in the Yung Ho Kung monastery in Peking, and once more we talked of the steppe life and the spirit of the wild. And he told me about Polycarpus's last journey.

He lies deep in the land of snow, in a cairn of sacred stones, over which, winter after winter, a new covering of snow and ice forms. In the short summer months Mohammedan and Buddhist pilgrims mutter their prayers when they pass the foreign pilgrim's grave, and when the white stillness of winter spreads over the heights, the sun of the Himalayas and the stars of the land of snow are mirrored in the crystal-clear glaciers under which he rests.

EAST IS EAST . . . ?

IN many of the States of the East the white man until quite recently occupied a privileged position. His compatriots had built up this position at a time when the population of these countries was divided into a small, all-powerful ruling class and a vast mass of sweating coolies, who had bowed themselves for so long under a heavy yoke that they had acquired many characteristics of the slave mentality.

The first white diplomatists and traders who came to the East sought contact, for obvious reasons, with the upper class of the country. To associate with that class as equals, the white men adopted many of its habits of life, and these were soon found to be so pleasant that they were transformed into necessities and formed the traditional standard of living in the white colonies in the East.

People lived in splendid bungalows and kept a large staff of servants, who treated their white masters with the deference due from a servant to his master in accordance with the old customs of the country. They are ideal servants, these Orientals, gliding noiselessly about in their white clothes to anticipate and fulfil their master's slightest wish. It is equally in accordance with the old customs of the country that a master never enters the isolated part of the house which contains the servants' private lives, and seldom learns to understand the thoughts hidden behind their shut faces.

One can live for a lifetime in the coast towns of the East without getting to know anything about the lower-class Chinese beyond the fact that he can be trained to become a perfect servant. He can be so efficient and reliable that both home and family are willingly left to his care; people even dare entrust their children's first tottering steps to the solicitude of the native *amah*.

Of course there have always been white men who did not follow the customary mode of life. There were the missionaries, who mingled with the native masses to convert them to the Christian religion; but many of these self-denying men were so convinced of the sacredness of their own doctrine and so certain of the unbelief of others, that all too often they concentrated their interest exclusively on the handful of the natives who unreservedly accepted their creed.

The white man who in the East was attracted into a native milieu simply to listen and understand, without making any attempt to reform or convert, had the label " gone native " affixed to him by his fellow-countrymen; and everyone who has been in the East knows how hopelessly declassed a man is to whom these words are applied. They signify that he has betrayed his race, deserted—that he has associated with a people with whom he should have had no intimate contact. He breaks with the social laws which his countrymen guard with holy zeal, and renounces all claim to their respect.

East and West may be the opposite poles of our earth, and no common thoroughfare has yet joined together the Eastern and Western worlds, so fundamentally different. But there are men and women who have listened more than they have preached, and understood more than they have condemned ; and their lives are incontrovertible proofs that warm relationships can be established between the worlds of East and West.

Time and time again I have discussed the question of " East and West ", and many, to support their doubts of the tenability of my views, have quoted Kipling's famous lines :

" Oh, East is East, and West is West, and never the twain shall meet,
Till Earth and Sky stand presently at God's great Judgment Seat. . ."

These introductory lines to the ballad, which bears witness to Kipling's profound understanding of men in both East and West, are twisted to prove the impossibility of finding a way to intimate contact between the peoples of East and West. But when, in discussion, I have asked for a continuation of the poem, and begged my opponent to reserve a little of his attention for the part of it that follows, which is its kernel, I have practically always found that he did not know how the ballad went on. When I myself have been able to complete his knowledge, this as a rule has altered the course of the discussion, for while certainly East is East and West is West, Kipling continues :

" But there is neither East nor West, Border, nor Breed, nor Birth,
When two strong men stand face to face, tho' they come from the ends of the earth ! "

" The white man's days in the East are numbered " were words often to be heard in the years before this war. When

I asked what these lugubrious words meant, I often found that the real grievance was the prospect of the days of privilege and luxury being terminated.

In my youth I enjoyed to the full the privileged existence of the Westerner in the East, and I understand the sorrow with which those who have grown accustomed to that pleasant and carefree life look forward to its cessation. But I do not think the world has cause to regret that the " days of the white man " in the East in that sense are disappearing—for ever. The foreign habits which the white men adopted were often the dross of a long obsolete culture, which they copied without considering that it had no solid foundation either in their own world or in the part of the world that was giving them hospitality.

I am glad that Providence took me away from the temptations of the China coast before I myself became rooted in its life ; and I am thankful for the day on which I rode through the Great Wall of China, out over the endless steppes of Mongolia, where I could follow fresh tracks and get to know a new life and new people in a milieu about which no one could instruct me, because no one knew it.

The Westerner who wishes to set off from the foreign colonies on the coast for the wild regions of Mongolia will have difficulty in getting any of his well-trained servants to accompany him. But if, despite this, he enters the nomads' country, he will soon have quite new experiences. He will meet a people which follows its chiefs as a matter of course with a fidelity to tradition which is far more loyal than any discipline maintained by force. But both chiefs and people live their roaming life in such close contact with the almighty forces of nature that they learn to judge their neighbour by his personal qualities rather than by his social position.

There are people who declare that the white man's days will soon be numbered in Mongolia too. A time of special privilege for the whites in Mongolia cannot disappear, for it has never existed. I have lived for many years among the nomads of Central Asia without ever feeling that the colour of my skin gave me any special rights to which my coloured companions were not equally entitled. I have lived there for months on end without ever giving a thought to the fact that I lived among bronze-coloured men and myself was white, and without the Mongols ever treating me as inferior to the best men of their own race. And I trust the Mongols, so long as they are spared much foreign civilization, to hold fast to their ancient custom of treating a foreigner as well as their own people, even if he is a white man.

It is a good thing if the foreigner in the nomad country quickly comes to understand this attitude of theirs, for it can help him over the consciousness of his own littleness that so often threatens to overpower him. On hunting trips on horseback he cannot but admire the close contact which his native companions have with Nature. In the desert he has often to trust his fate to their instinctive sense of direction, and he is ceaselessly obliged to seek their counsel in all vital questions of life in wild regions. He accepts from the natives every day help of such a kind that money cannot pay for it, and he looks forward to the day when he will be able to do a worthy service in return. And imperceptibly the day comes when the smiling nomads, from being friendly hosts, are transformed into confidential friends. When that day comes, one has taken root and feels at home in the nomad world.

He who accompanies the nomads on their journeyings through snow and sandstorms learns to admire the resignation with which they meet trouble on their road. He goes with them across the steppe in the luxuriance of summer, up to the view-points in the mountains, and envies them the fervency with which they take to their hearts all that is beautiful. And when, in evening hours rich in atmosphere, he meditates on the great experiences of the day and remembers the civilization of which he is a product, he feels that much of what we think we have grown out of and risen above in reality makes life richer.

I think it is easier for a Westerner to find harmony in Mongolia than in any other Eastern country. The steppe and its scenery are so wild and overwhelming, and the people are so few and live so far apart, that one quickly learns to stretch out one's hand in understanding and help.

There is a tendency to regard the nomads as savage barbarians, but not only have I found in their little felt tents shelter against the fury of Nature, protection against dangers, food and kindness, but they have, moreover, for years satisfied my ideas of home and home comfort. It is a happy time for me to look back upon ; they are firmly fixed in my memory, those hosts and travelling companions of mine, and I can see their weather-beaten faces, tried and tested by life, before me in the magic colours of the camp fires.

It is long since I stayed in Nirma's tent ; I was with her only three days, but I would gladly ride any distance to meet her once again. But Nirma must be dead long ago, and as she was the last of her family and lived alone in an out-of-the-way spot, I can certainly never expect to meet anyone with whom I can talk of her.

I had lost my way on horseback in Ala-shan's sea of sand ; my horse was exhausted, and silence, loneliness and thirst had worn out my nerves. Suddenly I caught sight of a poor old woman coming along, leading a goat. I think I embraced her in my delight, but she greeted my sudden appearance with the same restrained friendliness with which one greets an acquaintance on one's daily promenade. Not till she had led me to her tent, watered my horse and her own seven goats, and given me food and drink, did she sit down by my side to hear what news I had to bring from the great world to her distant water-hole.

I remained for three days in her lonely little tent, and she told me stories of the clouds in her sky, and crooned songs whose naive poetry illuminated her grey world of sand with its imaginative beauty.

When I was about to set off again, she gave me much good advice regarding my journey, and at the moment of farewell she took a little clay lamp from the poor altar table in the tent. It was her only lamp, and certainly the only one she ever would own ; but after she had taught me how to fill it with fat from a melted sheep's tail and make wicks of sheep's wool, she declared that it was mine. When I protested, she assured me that I had more use for it than she, for she had noticed that my young eyes did not see as well in the desert night as her old ones.

On many a long winter evening Nirma's lamp has shone for me, and it has thrown the bright warm light of understanding upon many of my experiences in Mongolia. For her East and West were two equally bright points upon her far-flung desert horizon.

INDEX

Aa Boulevard, 2
Abak, chief of, 117
Adochen tribe, 126, 172
Adventurers at Kalgan, 179-81
Afghanistan, 217
Ah Lin, 10-11
Ala-shan, 225
Albert, Uncle, 2-3
Alexander the Great, 210
Altai mountains, 132-3
Altan Khan, 112-13, 115, 117-18
Altan *Obo*, 145-51
American club at Ilo-ilo, 7-9
American Express Company, 7
Andrew Cross, 104
Antelopes, Orongo, 2
Asia Minor, 192
Avalanche, fall of, 218
Avo, 58, 62-3

Baante Hurel, 173
Babodjab, 182
Bactrian camels, 113
Bai Djyn-ying, 25-8, 30-5
Banche, 184-8
Bantje, 80-90
Barga steppe, 80
Batkhalag, 189
Bato-Merin, 153-8, 163-4
Bayan Dokhom, 172-4
Bears, bear-hunters, bears' meat, 83-6
Bejing, 182
Biliktai, 211-18
Bimba Noyen, 154-9, 161-2
" Black Mouse's Year ", 73-4
Blue City, 112-18, 189-90, 193 ; Mountain, 184-6

Bodachi, 52, 70
Bodaha tribes, 102
Bomberdi, 88
Boxer rebellion, 193, 195
Britain, British, 97, 209, 215
Buddha, Gotama, 212 ; " Living ", 132, 148-51 ; Sukya Muni, 214
Buddhism, 93-4, 112, 139-40, 194, 210
Budh Gaya, 212, 214
Buir-nor, 97-9
Bund (Shanghai), 16-17
Buriats, 113, 132-3
Burma, 216
Burzil pass, 217-18

Calcutta, 210-12, 216
Canton, 20
Cathay Hotel, 16
Cattle plague, 140-4
Central Empire, 14, 32
Chahar Mongols, 89, 141, 175, 177, 184-7
Chao, Colonel, 194-5
Chapser, 187
China, Chinese, 5, 10-11, 13-38, 44, 52-6, 60, 62, 66, 68-71, 73-4, 92-6, 102, 111-15, 117-18, 124, 126, 141, 177-8, 181-8, 191-6, 209-10, 221-2
China, Customs, 15-17 ; Great Wall, 44, 93, 111, 114-15, 118, 177-8, 187, 190, 192-3, 223 ; Sea, 6, 9, 12-13, 15, 18-21 ; Steam Navigation Co., 13

227

INDEX

Chinese Christians, 194-6 ;
colonization, 36, 96, 115 ;
Republic, 95, 114-15, 117-18, 186
Compradors, 17
Compressed tea, 46, 135
Congo, 2-3
Copenhagen, 2, 215-16
Cossacks, 102-5
Christian colonies, 180 ; rule in Central Asia, 190-2
Christians, Chinese, 194-6 ; Nestorian, 191-3, 196
Craftsmen, Manchurian, 55-7, 63
Crusaders, 191

Damarin Surong, 185
Dannebrog, 215
Darkhan, 129
Darkhan Beil Mongols, 141
Delevar Gegen, 148-51
Delhi, 213, 216
Demchik, 132-3, 135
Demchik Dorche, 118
Denmark, visitor from, 215
Desert, lure of, 1, 199 ; Gobi, 126 ; Ordos, 119-20, 190 ; Taklamakan, 198-9
Devil dance, 71, 76-7
Djalserai, 132-3
Djangsara Anga, 66
Djirimtai, 108-9
Dolo Nor, 79
Dongche monastery, 213-17
Dragon Prince, 139-40, 143, 146, 166
Dragon Throne, 32, 52, 54, 69-70, 94, 111, 113-14
Duke Larson, 141, 181
Dundurdjab, 38
Durbet, 189
Dzitker, 168

" East and West ", 220-6
Eastern Mongolia, 51, 96-7
Eastern servants, 221, 223
Emperor K'ang Hsi, 69, 72-3 ; Tao Kwang, 32 ; of Franks, 191 ; of Manchukuo, 96
Empress Dowager (Tzu Hsi), 69, 193-4
Eredin Monke, 161
Erh Fu, Princess, 52-7, 63
Eriksson, Dr Joel, 141
Erlik Khan, 167-8
Estrangelo inscriptions, 190
Etsin Horo, 119
Everest, 209

Feng Chia Yuan, 26-35
Feng family, 26, 32
Filipinos, 7-9
Fire customs, 122-31, 135-8
Fire-god, 125-31
" Fire Maiden, Holy ", 133-8
Forbidden City, 26, 32, 52-5, 68-9
" Forty-seven passes ", 52, 55
Franks, Emperors of, 191
Franzon, Fr, 192
Fukien, 13

Gandara style, 210
Gauri Sankar, 209, 213
Gaz Köl, 2
Geishas, 106
Gill, Julia, 11
Gobi, 126
" Gone native ", 221
" Golden Khan ", 112-13, 115, 117-18, 192 ; " Obo ", 145-51
Gongerer, 65, 67
Gotama Buddha, 212
Græda Merin, 60-2, 65

INDEX

Great Wall of China, 44, 93, 111, 114-15, 118, 177-8, 187, 190, 192-3, 223
Greenland, 99
Gurtum, 75-7

Haikh-Lama, 168-75
Hailar, 102-6
Hainan, 14-15, 17-18, 20-1
Haisan, 89
Hangan, Lake, 89-90
" Heaven-worshipping father", 154-9, 161-2, 164
Hedin, Sven, 199
Himalayas, 38, 209, 213-19
" Holy Fire Maiden ", 133-8
Hongkong, 4-5, 9-12 ; and Shanghai Bank, 16
Hotel de Peking, 24-5 ; Rome (Hailar), 104
Hsingan, 36-7, 82, 89, 102
Hsingan-Mongolia, 36, 96
Hsi-pei feng, 25
Hugtjo Bo, 91, 99
Hunters, twelve, 49-51, 56-8
Hurum, 153-64
Hutungs of Peking, 25, 27-31

Ikhe Bator, 87
Ilo-ilo, 5-9
India, 208-13
Inner Mongolia, 115, 140-1, 187
" Island of Palms ", 14-15, 17, 20-21

Jabonah, 78
Japan, Japanese, 37, 39-40, 62, 66, 96-8, 102-3, 106, 109, 187, 216 ; occupation of Manchuria, 96, 102-3, 187
Jasaktu Mongols, 36-58

Java Sea, 6
Jehol, 44
Jenghiz Khan, 44, 70, 87, 91-3, 99, 117, 119, 124, 126, 128-9, 141, 210
Jeremiassen, Carl C., 14-15, 17-21
Jeruke mountain, 42-5, 52
Jeshigema, 170-5
Jetom, 132-3
John, Presbyter (Prester), 191-2
John Little's bar, 5
Julia Gill, 11
Jyrul, 174

Kalgan, 167, 179-81, 184, 187, 212
Kanbalu, 199
K'ang Hsi, 69
Kansu, 180, 214
Kashgaria, 26, 212
Kashmir, 213
Kazan Cossacks, 105
Keraits, 191-2
Keshikt country, 81
Khabto Khasar, 44-5, 51-2, 57, 70-2, 87
Khalkha, 148 ; Mongols 113
" Khara Holerens Djil ", 73-4
Khara Korum, 92
Khatun Sume, 41, 48-58
Khorchin, 44, 52, 59, 61-3, 69-74
Khotan, 113 ; carpet, 197, 202
Khukhu Khoto, 112
" King George ", 191
" King's Monastery ", 71-8
Kipling, 222
Kirgises, 113
Kolchak, Admiral, 95
Kowloon, 5, 10-12
Kumiss, 64-5, 85
Kurban Beg, 197, 200, 203-6

INDEX

Kwangtung, 13
Kwei Sui, 112

Ladakh, 213
Lamadjab, 47-52, 56-7, 71, 77-9
Lamaism, 93-4, 97, 105, 125, 139, 170, 192, 214
Larson, Duke, 141, 181
Lenox Simpson, 26-7
Leopold II, 2
Leopoldville, 2
Lhasa, 97, 212
Li, 27-35
Li Chouw Hsin, 182
Lindquist, Polycarpus, 215-19
" Lions' Island ", 4
Little, John, 5
" Living Buddha ", 132, 148-51
Lodou, 184

Macedonians, 210
MacGregor, Captain, 18-21 ; Mr and Mrs, 18, 21
Magellan, 6
Manchu Ail, 58-67, 71
Manchu dynasty, 52, 54, 68, 77, 94-5, 113, 117, 186 ; Mongols, 63
Manchukuo, 36-7, 96 ; Emperor of, 96
Manchuria, Japanese occupation of, 96, 102-3, 187
Manchurian craftsmen, 55-7, 63 ; princess, 68-71
Manila, 5
Marco Polo, 121, 191, 199
Martin, 191
Mecca, 214
Medek hung, 127-30
Methodist Mission, 14-15
Mikado, 104

Ming dynasty, 52, 94, 112-13
Mission, Methodist, 14-15 ; Swedish Alliance, 192, 194-6 ; Swedish Mongolia, 141, 192
Missionaries, murder of, 193
Modji-Yamen, 37-9
Mohammedans, 105-6, 115-16, 118, 191, 194, 197, 202, 214
Monasteries, 93-5, 97, 178
Monastery, Dongche, 213-16 ; " the King's ", 71-8 ; Yung Ho Kung, 218
Mongoldjin, 182
Mongolia, Eastern, 51, 96-7 ; Inner, 115, 140-1 ; Northern, 81, 115, 192, 212 ; Outer, 95 ; Southern, 140, 177
Mongolian chronicles, 98 ; language, 96-7
Monsoon, 208
" Mountain Goat Pass ", 71
" Mountains of Gold ", 133
Mundi, 132
" Muses' Stream ", 59-60

Naidung Djalan, 80, 84-6, 88-9
Naidung Taichi, 153
Namserai, 72, 74-7
Nan Sheng, 36
Nanga Tarbat, 209
Nestorian Christians, 191-3, 196
" New City ", 112-18
New Time, 45, 99, 175
New York City Bank, 7
Nicholas, St, 143-4
Nija, girls from, 202-7
" Nine Dragons ", 10
Nirma, 225-6

INDEX

Northern Mongolia, 81, 115, 192, 212
Nukodar, Empress, 217

Oasis, visit to, 197-207
Obos, 42-5, 140, 144-51, 167
Odei Wang, 38, 40
Old Man of the Steppe, White, 139-40, 143-5, 166
Olsen, Emanuel, 192
Olympic Games, 144
Ordos desert, 119-20, 190
Orion, 107
Orongo antelopes, 2
Outer Mongolia, 95

Pacific Ocean, 210
Pao Tun-ling, 182, 187
Peking, 20, 22-35, 68-71, 92, 94, 113, 186, 194, 205, 218
Persian fire-worshippers, 121-2
Philippines, 6-9
Pilgrims, 212, 214
Pioneer tavern, 179-80
Pirates, 7, 19-21
Polycarpus Lindquist, 215-19
Popes, 191
Presbyter (Prester) John, 191-2
Princess Erh Fu, 52-7, 63; Shou Shan Yü, 68-71, 78-9
Princess's temple, 41, 48-58
Princesses, Siamese, 5-6
Przhevalski, 199
Puntsuk, 37-57

Queen Victoria, 10

Raadhusplads, 216
Raffles, 6
Rawalpindi, 216
Red Army, 95; Guards, 178
Republic, Chinese, 95, 114-15, 177-8, 186

" River of wealth ", 59
Robbers, frontier, 38, 181-8
Rositta, 9
Rue de la Paix, 18
Russia, Soviet, 95, 102, 178, 209, 214; Tsarist, 95, 103, 178

Saadgum, Prince, 52-7
Sain-bayer, 182, 187-8
St John's Eve, 144
St Nicholas, 143-4
Sanang Setsen, 98
Sangerup, 40-1, 43, 50, 59-63, 71-7, 80-6
Sarts, Sartish, 113, 203
Sassoon House, 16
Scandinavia, 99, 109, 143-4
Schiolma, 168
Sha-Beis, 147-8, 151
Shaman, 194
Shanghai, 4-5, 12, 16-22
Shibchin tribes, 102
Shou Shan Yü, Princess, 68-71, 78-9
Shur-tsisik, 89-90
Siam, 216; King of, 5; princesses, 5-6
Siberia, 44, 102, 113, 178
Siberian Cossacks, 103-4
Simpson, Lenox, 26-7
Singapore, 4-6
Sining, 113
Sjagder, 126-31
Skaane, 194, 196
Söderbom, Georg, 141-6, 191
Solon, 36, 59, 62, 102
Son of Heaven, 52
South China Sea, 18-19
Southern Cross, 6, 9
Southern Mongolia, 140, 177
Soviet Union, 95, 102, 178, 214
Srinagar, 216-17

INDEX

Standard Oil Company, 7
Stanley, 2
Statue of Liberty, 212
Stein, Sir Aurel, 199
Street traders in Peking, 28, 30
Sui-yuan, 112-18
Sulo Sea, 6
Su-mu-ling, 177, 183-8
Sunit Mongols, 89, 141
Surong, 81-3, 86-7
Swedish Alliance Mission, 192 ; Mongolia Mission, 141, 192 ; missionaries, murder of, 193

Taipans, 17
Taklamakan, 198-9
Tamerlane, 210
Tantra religion, 212
Tao Kwang, Emperor, 32
Taonan-Solon railway, 36
Tartar city, 25, 27
Tartars, Tartary, 44, 191
Teh Wang, 117-18, 140-1
Tenduc, 191
" Three Lanterns Pass ", 60
Tibet, 2, 93, 112-13, 115, 126, 169, 190, 206-7
Tientsin, 210
Todbadjamso, 52, 54-5
Tokhto, 191
Torgon Sjare, 126, 128
Torgut pilgrims, 212
Tragbal pass, 217
Trans-Baikal Cossacks, 104
Trans-Manchurian Railway, 36, 102
Trengganu, 5
Troubadours, 159
Tsaran Geril, 165-75
Tsarist Russia, 95, 103, 178
Tumet Mongols, 89, 112-13, 117, 141, 192

Tungans, 104, 113
Tunguses, 57
Turfan wine, 203
Turkestan, 113, 115, 126, 190, 204, 213, 215, 217
Turkmenians, 212, 214
Turks, 191
Tut, 168
Tzu Hsi, Empress Dowager, 69, 193-4

Uncle Albert, 2-3
Ungern, Baron, 95, 178
Urga, 211-12

" Valley of the Scented Waters ", 5, 10
Vancouver, 210, 213
Victoria, Queen, 10 ; Club, 10

Wagon Lits Hotel, 23-4
Wall of China, Great, 44, 93, 111, 114-15, 118, 177-8, 187, 190, 192-3, 223
Wang, Pastor, 195-6
Wang-yeh Miao, 36-40
Water Gate, 23
Wedding feast, 153-64
White Guards, 95, 102, 178
White man in the East, 220-6
White Old Man of the Steppe, 139-40, 143-5, 166
Wibergs, 194-6
" Wild Goat Pass ", 206
Wolves, attack by, 107-9
Wu, General, 74 ; rickshaw man, 23-4

Yangtse, 16
Yarkand, 212-13, 217
Yellow River, 119
Yung Ho Kung Monastery, 218

Zooji-la, 213, 217

PLATE I

Manchu Princess

PLATE II

Mongol Chief

PLATE III

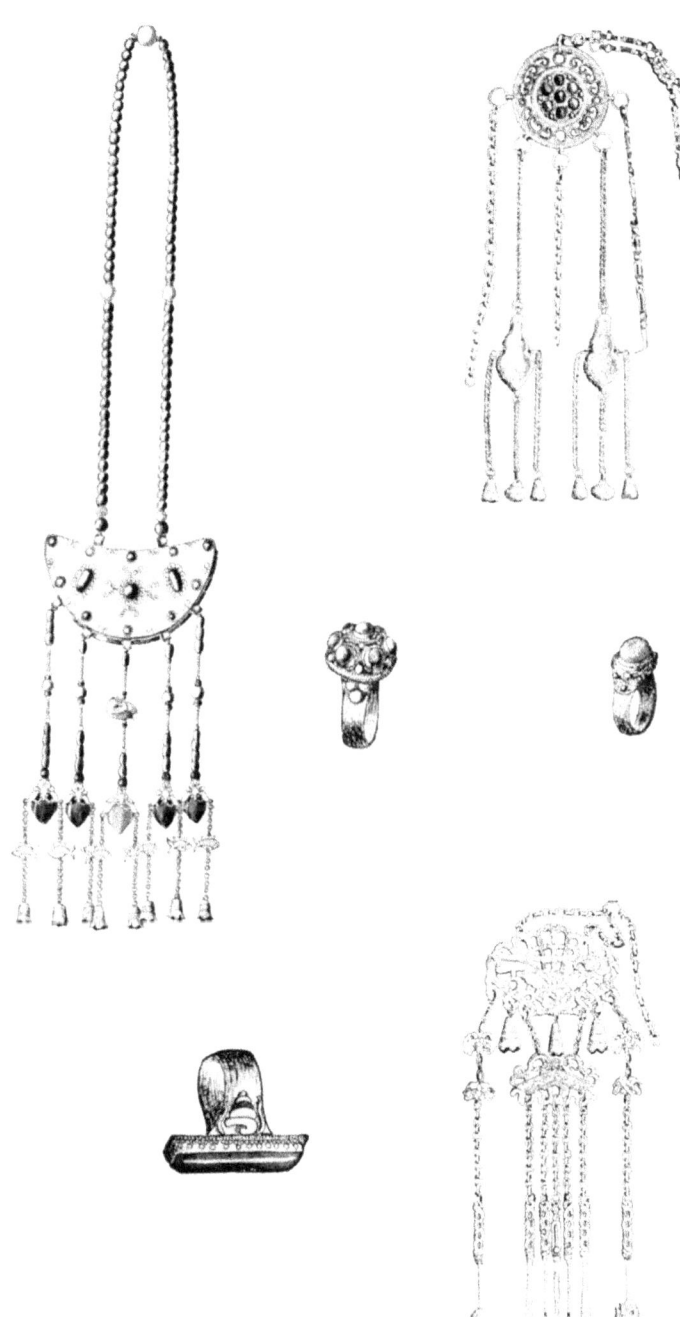

A Bride's Dowry (i)

PLATE IV

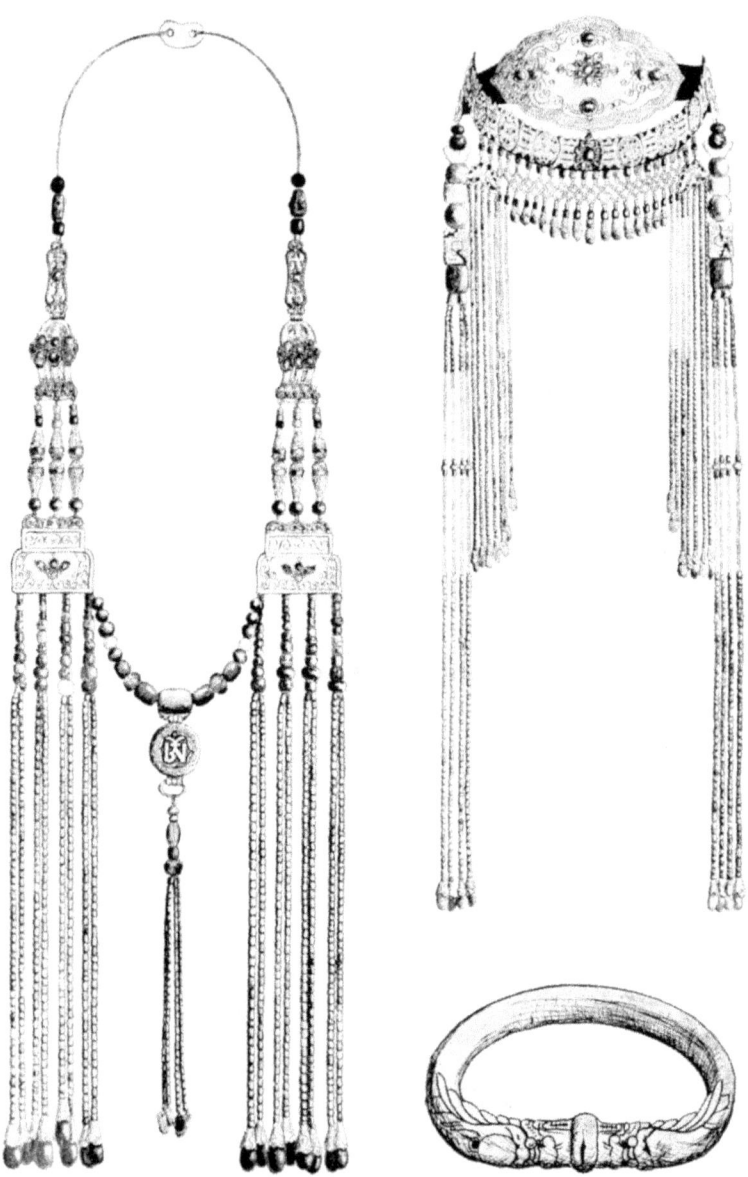

A Bride's Dowry (ii)

PLATE V

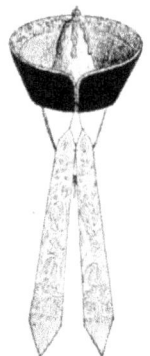

A Bride's Dowry (iii)

PLATE VI

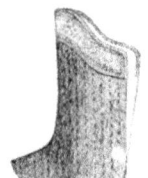

A Bride's Dowry (iv)

PLATE VII

Warrior

Troubadour

Shepherd

Shepherdess

PLATE VIII

Story-teller

Bowman

Lama

Pilgrim

PLATE IX

Headman of Camp

Wife

Son

Daughter-in-law

PLATE X

Unmarried Girl

The Younger Generation

Caravan Leader

Hunter

PLATE XI

Novice

Haikh-Lama

Gurtum

The Girl from Nija

PLATE XII

The White Old Man of the Steppe

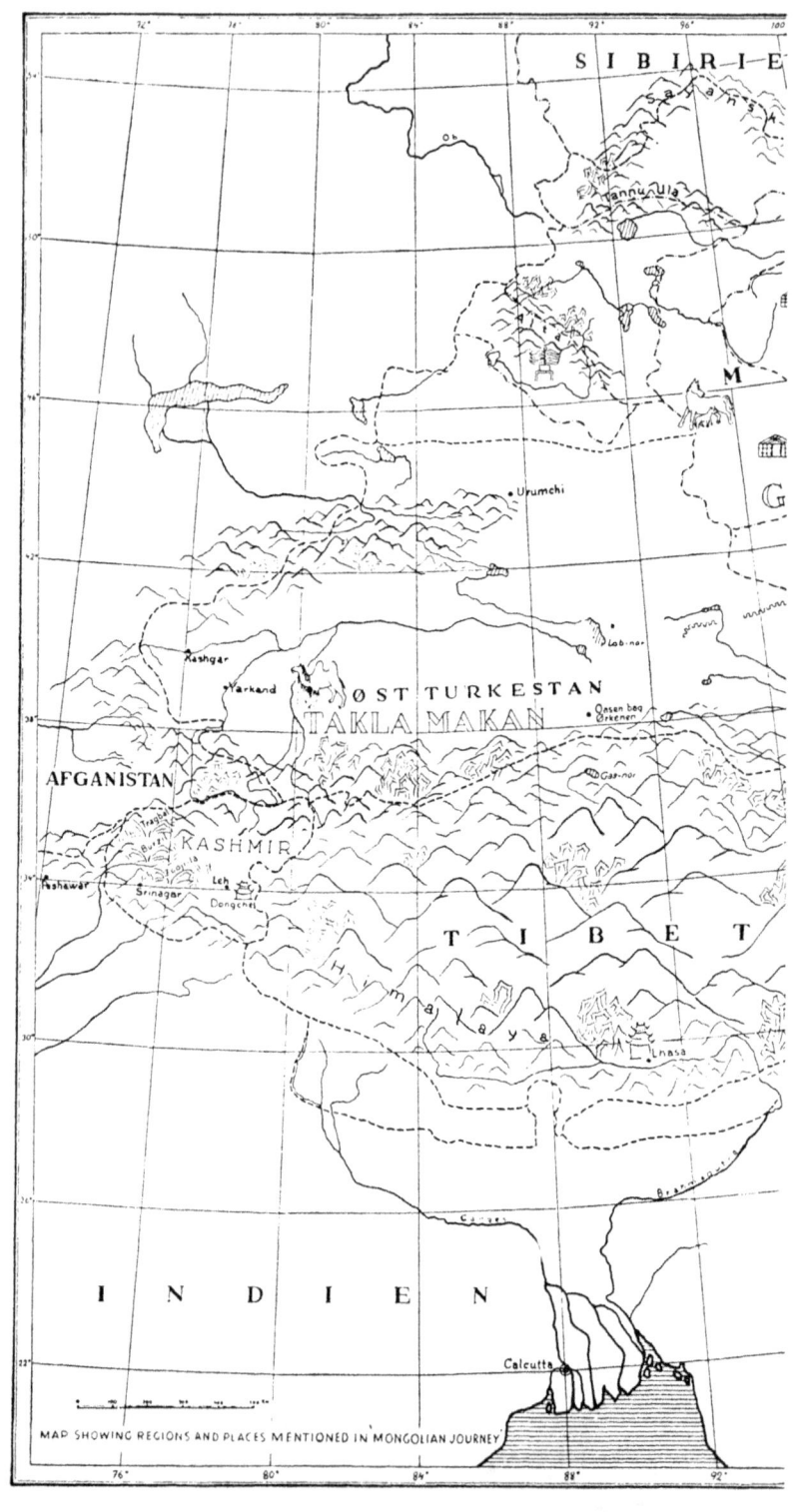

MAP SHOWING REGIONS AND PLACES MENTIONED IN MONGOLIAN JOURNEY

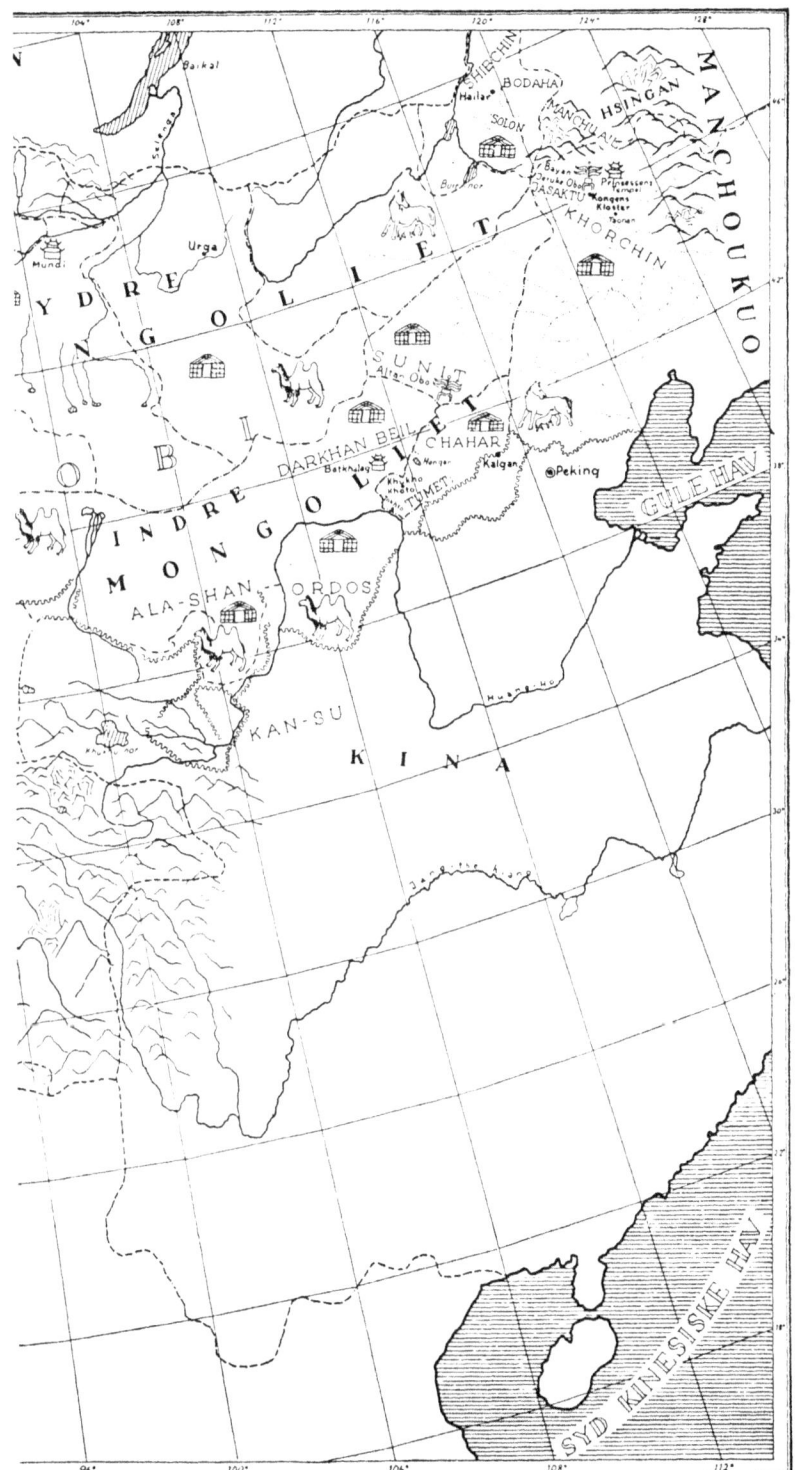

For Product Safety Concerns and Information please contact our EU representative GPSR@taylorandfrancis.com
Taylor & Francis Verlag GmbH, Kaufingerstraße 24, 80331 München, Germany

www.ingramcontent.com/pod-product-compliance
Lightning Source LLC
Chambersburg PA
CBHW071820300426
44116CB00009B/1385